Good Newes
from
New England

Map of Plymouth from Young's *Chronicles*

WINSLOW'S RELATION.

Good Newes
from
New England

A TRUE RELATION OF THINGS VERY REMARKABLE AT
THE PLANTATION OF PLIMOTH IN NEW ENGLAND.

BY EDWARD WINSLOW

APPLEWOOD BOOKS
BEDFORD, MASSACHUSETTS

Good Newes from New England was first published in 1624.

Cover photograph courtesy of Plimoth Plantation Inc.

Thank you for purchasing an Applewood Book.
Applewood reprints America's lively classics —books
from the past that are still of interest to modern readers.
For a free copy of our current catalog, please write to:
Applewood Books, P.O. Box 365, Bedford, MA 01730.

ISBN 1-55709-443-8

Printed in the United States of America.

Library of Congress Catalog Card Number: 96–85204

WINSLOW'S RELATION.

"GOOD NEWES FROM NEW ENGLAND: or a true Relation of
  things very remarkable at the Plantation of *Plimoth* in New-
  England.
Shewing the wondrous providence and goodness of GOD, in their
  preservation and continuance, being delivered from many
  apparent deaths and dangers.
Together with a Relation of such religious and civill Lawes and
  Customes, as are in practise amongst the *Indians*, adjoyning to
  them at this day. As also what Commodities are there to be
  raysed for the maintenance of that and other Plantations
  in the said Country.
Written by *E. W.* who hath borne a part in the fore-named
  troubles, and there lived since their first Arrivall.
Whereunto is added by him a briefe Relation of a credible
  intelligence of the present Estate of *Virginia.*
LONDON. Printed by *I. D.* for *William Bladen* and *Iohn Bellamie,*
  and are to be sold at their Shops, at the *Bible* in *Paul's* Church-
  yard, and at the three Golden Lyons in Corn-hill, neere the
  Royall Exchange. 1624." pp. 66, sm. 4to.

DEDICATION

To all well-willers and furtherers of Plantations in New England,
especially to such as ever have or desire to assist the people of Plymouth
in their just proceedings, grace and peace be multiplied.

RIGHT HONORABLE AND WORSHIPFUL
    GENTLEMEN, OR WHATSOEVER,

S INCE it hath pleased God to stir you up to be instruments of
his glory in so honorable an enterprise as the enlarging of his
Majesty's dominions by planting his loyal subjects in so
healthful and hopeful a country as New-England is, where the
church of God being seated in sincerity, there is no less hope of
convincing the heathen of their evil ways, and converting them to
the true knowledge and worship of the living God, and so consequently the salvation of their souls by the merits of Jesus Christ,
than elsewhere, though it be much talked on and lightly or lamely
prosecuted, – I therefore think it but my duty to offer the view of
our proceedings to your worthy considerations, having to that end
composed them together thus briefly, as you see; wherein, to your
great encouragement, you may behold the good providence of
God working with you in our preservation from so many dangerous plots and treacheries as have been intended against us, as also
in giving his blessing so powerfully upon the weak means we had,
enabling us with health and ability beyond expectation in our
greatest scarcities, and possessing the hearts of the salvages with
astonishment and fear of us; whereas if God had let them loose,
they might easily have swallowed us up, scarce being a handful in
comparison of those forces they might have gathered together
against us; which now, by God's blessing, will be more hard and
difficult, in regard our number of men is increased, our town better fortified, and our store better victualled. Blessed therefore be

3

his name, that hath done so great things for us and hath wrought so great a change amongst us.

Accept, I pray you, my weak endeavours, pardon my unskilfulness, and bear with my plainness in the things I have handled. Be not discouraged by our former necessities, but rather encouraged with us, hoping that God hath wrought with us in our beginning of this worthy work, undertaken in his name and fear, so he will by us accomplish the same to his glory and our comfort, if we neglect not the means. I confess it hath not been much less chargeable to some of you[1] than hard and difficult to us, that have endured the brunt of the battle, and yet small profits returned. Only, by God's mercy, we are safely seated, housed, and fortified, by which means a great step is made unto gain, and a more direct course taken for the same, than if at first we had rashly and covetously fallen upon it.

Indeed three things are the overthrow and bane, as I may term it, of plantations.

1. The vain expectation of present profit, which too commonly taketh a principal seat in the heart and affection, though God's glory, &c. is preferred before it in the mouth with protestation.

2. Ambition in their governors and commanders, seeking only to make themselves great, and slaves of all that are under them, to maintain a transitory base honor in themselves, which God oft punisheth with contempt.

3. The carelessness of those that send over supplies of men unto them, not caring how they be qualified; so that ofttimes they are rather the image of men endued with bestial, yea, diabolical affections, than the image of God, endued with reason, understanding, and holiness. I praise God I speak not these things experimentally, by way of complaint of our own condition, but having great cause on the contrary part to be thankful to God for his mercies towards us; but rather, if there be any too desirous of gain, to entreat them to moderate their affections, and consider that no man expecteth fruit before the tree be grown; advising all men, that as they tender their

own welfare, so to make choice of such to manage and govern their affairs, as are approved not to be seekers of themselves, but the common good of all for whom they are employed; and beseeching such as have the care of transporting men for the supply and furnishing of plantations, to be truly careful in sending such as may further and not hinder so good an action. There is no godly, honest man but will be helpful in his kind, and adorn his profession with an upright life and conversation; which doctrine of manners[2] ought first to be preached by giving good example to the poor savage heathens amongst whom they live. On the contrary part, what great offence hath been given by many profane men, who being but seeming Christians, have made Christ and Christianity stink in the nostrils of the poor infidels, and so laid a stumbling-block before them. But woe be to them by whom such offences come.

These things I offer to your Christian considerations, beseeching you to make a good construction of my simple meaning, and take in good part this ensuing Relation, dedicating myself and it evermore unto your service; beseeching God to crown our Christian and faithful endeavours with his blessings temporal and eternal.

Yours in this service,
Ever to be commanded,
E. W.[3]

TO THE READER.

GOOD READER,

WHEN I first penned this Discourse, I intended it chiefly for the satisfaction of my private friends; but since that time have been persuaded to publish the same. And the rather, because of a disorderly colony[1] that are dispersed, and most of them returned, to the great prejudice and damage of him[2] that set them forth; who, as they were a stain to Old England that bred them, in respect of their lives and manners amongst the Indians, so, it is to be feared, will be no less to New England, in their vile and clamorous reports, because she would not foster them in their desired idle courses. I would not be understood to think there were no well deserving persons amongst them; for of mine knowledge it was a grief to some that they were so yoked; whose deserts, as they were then suitable to their honest protestations, so I desire still may be in respect of their just and true Relations.

Peradventure thou wilt rather marvel that I deal so plainly, than any way doubt of the truth of this my Relation; yea, it may be, tax me therewith, as seeming rather to discourage men than any way to further so noble an action. If any honest mind be discouraged, I am sorry. Sure I am I have given no just cause; and am so far from being discouraged myself, as I purpose to return forthwith.[3] And for other light and vain persons, if they stumble hereat, I have my desire, accounting it better for them and us that they keep where they are, as being unfit and unable to perform so great a task.

Some faults have escaped because I could not attend on the press,[4] which I pray thee correct, as thou findest, and I shall account it as a favor unto me.

Thine,

E. W.

Chapter 1

A BRIEF RELATION OF A CREDIBLE INTELLIGENCE OF THE PRESENT ESTATE OF VIRGINIA.

AT the earnest entreaty of some of my much respected friends, I have added to the former Discourse a Relation of such things as were credibly reported at Plymouth, in New England, in September last past, concerning the present estate of Virginia. And because men may doubt how we should have intelligence of their affairs, being we are so far distant, I will therefore satisfy the doubtful therein. Captain Francis West[1] being in New England about the latter end of May past, sailed from thence to Virginia, and returned in August. In September the same ship and company being discharged by him at Damarin's Cove,[2] came to New Plymouth, where, upon our earnest inquiry after the state of Virginia since that bloody slaughter committed by the Indians upon our friends and countrymen,[3] the whole ship's company agreed in this, viz. that upon all occasions they chased the Indians to and fro, insomuch as they sued daily unto the English for peace, who for the present would not admit of any; that Sir George Early, &c. was at that present employed upon service against them; that amongst many other, Opachancano,[4] the chief emperor, was supposed to be slain; his son also was killed at the same time. And though, by reason of these forenamed broils in the fore part of the year, the English had undergone great want of food, yet, through God's mercy, there never was more show of plenty, having as much and as good corn on the ground as ever they had. Neither was the hopes of their tobacco crop inferior to that of their corn; so that the planters were never more full of encouragement; which I pray God long to continue, and so to direct both them and us, as his glory may be the principal aim and end of all our actions, and that for his mercy's sake. Amen.

Chapter 2

OF THEIR BEING MENACED BY THE
NARRAGANSETTS, AND THEIR SECOND
VOYAGE TO THE MASSACHUSETTS.

1622

THE good ship called the FORTUNE, which, in the month of November, 1621, (blessed be God,) brought us a new supply of thirty-five persons, was not long departed our coast, ere the great people of Nanohigganset,[1] which are reported to be many thousands strong, began to breathe forth many threats against us, notwithstanding their desired and obtained peace with us in the foregoing summer; insomuch as the common talk of our neighbour Indians on all sides was of the preparation they made to come against us. In reason a man would think they should have now more cause to fear us than before our supply came. But though none of them were present, yet understanding by others that they neither brought arms, nor other provisions with them, but wholly relied on us, it occasioned them to slight and brave us with so many threats as they did.[2] At length came one of them to us, who was sent by Conanacus,[3] their chief sachim or king, accompanied with one Tokamahamon, a friendly Indian. This messenger inquired for Tisquantum, our interpreter, who not being at home, seemed rather to be glad than sorry, and leaving for him a bundle of new arrows, lapped in a rattlesnake's skin, desired to depart with all expedition. But our governors not kowing what to make of this strange carriage, and comparing it with that we had formerly heard, committed him to the custody of Captain Standish, hoping now to know some certainty of that we so often heard, either by his own relation to us, or to Tisquantum, at his return, desiring myself, having special familiarity with the other forenamed Indian, to see if I could learn any thing from him; whose answer was sparingly to this effect, that he could not certainly tell us, but thought they were enemies to us.

Jan. That night Captain Standish gave me and another[4]
1622 charge of him, and gave us order to use him kindly, and
that he should not want any thing he desired, and to take
all occasions to talk and inquire of the reasons of those reports we
heard, and withal to signify that upon his true relation he should
be sure of his own freedom. At first, fear so possessed him that he
could scarce say any thing; but in the end became more familiar,
and told us that the messenger which his master sent in summer to
treat of peace, at his return persuaded him rather to war; and to the
end he might provoke him thereunto, (as appeared to him by our
reports,) detained many of the things [which] were sent him by or
Governor, scorning the meanness of them both in respect of what
himself had formerly sent, and also of the greatness of his own person; so that he much blamed the former messenger, saying, that
upon the knowledge of this his false carriage, it would cost him his
life, but assured us that upon his relation of our speech then with
him to his master, he would be friends with us. Of this we informed
the Governor and his Assistant[5] and Captain Standish, who, after
consultation, considered him howsoever but in the state of a messenger; and it being as well against the law of arms amongst them
as us in Europe to lay violent hands on any such, set him at liberty; the Governor giving him order to certify his master that he had
heard of his large and many threatenings, at which he was much
offended; daring him in those respects to the utmost, if he would
not be reconciled to live peaceably, as other his neighbours; manifesting withal (as ever) his desire of peace, but his fearless resolution, if he could not so live amongst them. After which he caused
meat to be offered him; but he refused to eat, making all speed to
return, and giving many thanks for his liberty, but requesting the
other Indian again to return. The weather being violent, he used
many words to persuade him to stay longer, but could not.
Whereupon he left him, and said he was with his friends, and
would not take a journey in such extremity.

After this, when Tisquantum returned, and the arrows were delivered, and the manner of the messenger's carriage related, he signified to the Governor that to send the rattlesnake's skin in that manner imported enmity, and that it was no better than a challenge.[6] Hereupon, after some deliberation, the Governor stuffed the skin with powder and shot, and sent it back, returning no less defiance to Conanacus, assuring him if he had shipping now present, thereby to send his men to Nanohigganset, (the place of his abode,) they should not need to come so far by land to us; yet withal showing that they should never come unwelcome or unlooked for. This message was sent by an Indian, and delivered in such sort, as it was no small terror to this savage king; insomuch as he would not once touch the powder and shot, or suffer it to stay in his house or country. Whereupon the messenger refusing it, another took it up; and having been posted from place to place a long time, at length came whole back again.

Feb. In the mean time, knowing our own weakness, notwith-
1622 standing our high words and lofty looks towards them, and still lying open to all casualty, having as yet (under God) no other defence than our arms, we thought it most needful to impale our town; which with all expedition we accomplished in the month of February, and some few days, taking in the top of the hill under which our town is seated; making four bulwarks or jetties without the ordinary circuit of the pale, from whence we could defend the whole town; in three whereof are gates,[7] and the fourth in time to be. This being done, Captain Standish divided our strength into four squadrons or companies, appointing whom he thought most fit to have command of each; and, at a general muster of training,[8] appointed each his place, gave each his company, giving them charge, upon every alarm, to resort to their leaders to their appointed place, and, in his absence, to be commanded and directed by them. That done according to his order, each drew his company to his appointed place for defence, and there together discharged their muskets. After which

they brought their new commanders to their houses, where again they graced them with their shot, and so departed.

Fearing, also, lest the enemy at any time should take any advantage by firing our houses, Captain Standish appointed a certain company, that whensoever they saw or heard fire to be cried in the town, should only betake themselves to their arms, and should enclose the house or place so endangered, and stand aloof on their guard, with their backs towards the fire, to prevent treachery, if any were in that kind intended. If the fire were in any of the houses of this guard, they were then freed from it; but not otherwise, without special command.

Mar. Long before this time we promised the people of 1622 Massachusets, in the beginning of March to come unto them, and trade for their furs; which being then come, we began to make preparation for that voyage. In the mean time, an Indian, called Hobbamock, who still lived in the town, told us that he feared the Massachusets or Massachuseucks (for so they called the people of that place,) were joined in confederacy with the Nanohigganeucks, or people of Nanohigganset, and that they therefore would take this opportunity to cut off Captain Standish and his company abroad; but, howsoever, in the mean time, it was to be feared that the Nanohigganeucks would assault the town at home; giving many reasons for his jealousy, as also that Tisquantum was in the confederacy, who, we should find, would use many persuasions to draw us from our shallops to the Indians' houses, for their better advantage. To confirm this his jealousy, he told us of many secret passages that passed between him and others, having their meetings ordinarily abroad, in the woods; but if at home, howsoever, he was excluded from their secrecy; saying it was the manner of the Indians, when they meant plainly, to deal openly; but in this his practice there was no show of honesty.

Hereupon the Governor, together with his Assistant and Captain Standish, called together such as by them were thought most meet for advice in so weighty a business; who, after consideration hereof, came to this resolution; that as hitherto, upon all occasions between them and us, we had ever manifested undaunted courage and resolution, so it would not now stand with our safety to mew up ourselves in our new-enclosed town; partly because our store was almost empty, and therefore must seek out for our daily food, without which we could not long subsist; but especially for that thereby they would see us dismayed, and be encouraged to prosecute their malicious purposes with more eagerness than ever they intended. Whereas, on the contrary, by the blessing of God, our fearless carriage might be a means to discourage and weaken their proceedings. And therefore thought best to proceed in our trading voyage, making this use of that we heard, to go the better provided, and use the more carefulness both at home and abroad, leaving the event to the disposing of the Almighty; whose providence, as it had hitherto been over us for good, so we had now no cause (save our sins) to despair of his mercy in our preservation and continuance, where we desired rather to be instruments of good to the heathens about us than to give them the least measure of just offence.

April. All things being now in readiness, the forenamed Captain, 1622 with ten men, accompanied with Tisquantum and Hobbamock, set forwards for the Massachusets. But we[9] had no sooner turned the point of the harbour, called the Gurnet's Nose,[10] (where, being becalmed, we let fall our grapnel to set things to right and prepare to row,) but there came an Indian of Tisquantum's family running to certain of our people that were from home with all eagerness, having his face wounded, and the blood still fresh on the same, calling to them to repair home, oft looking behind him, as if some others had him in chase; saying that at Namaschet (a town some fifteen miles from us,) there were many of the Nanohiggansets, Massassowat[11] our supposed friend, and Conbatant,[12] our feared enemy, with many others, with a resolution

April. to take advantage on the present opportunity to assault
1622 the town in the Captain's absence; affirming that he
       received the wound in his face for speaking in our behalf,
and by sleight escaped; looking oft backward, as if he suspected
them to be at hand. This he affirmed again to the Governor; whereupon he gave command that three pieces of ordnance should be
made ready and discharged, to the end that if we were not out of
hearing, we might return thereat; which we no sooner heard, but
we repaired homeward with all convenient speed, arming ourselves, and making all in readiness to fight. When we entered the
harbour, we saw the town likewise on their guard, whither we hast-
ed with all convenient speed. The news being made known unto
us, Hobbamock said flatly that it was false, assuring us of
Massassowat's faithfulness. Howsoever, he presumed he would
never have undertaken any such act without his privity, himself
being a *pinse*,[13] that is, one of his chiefest champions or men of
valor; it being the manner amongst them no to undertake such
enterprises without the advice and furtherance of men of that rank.
To this the Governor answered, he should be sorry that any just and
necessary occasions of war should arise between him and any [of]
the savages, but especially Massassowat; not that he feared him
more than the rest, but because his love more exceeded towards
him than any. Whereunto Hobbamock replied, there was no cause
wherefore he should distrust him, and therefore should do well to
continue his affections.

     But to the end things might be made more manifest, the
Governor caused Hobbamock to send his wife with all privacy to
Puckanokick, the chief place of Massassowat's residence, (pretending other occasions,) there to inform herself, and so us, of
the right state of things. When she came thither, and saw all
things quiet, and that no such matter was or had been intended,
[she] told Massassowat what had happened at Plymouth, (by
them called Patuxet;) which, when he understood, he was much

April. offended at the carriage of Tisquantum, returning many
1622 thanks to the Governor for his good thoughts of him,
and assuring him that, according to their first Articles of
Peace, he would send word and give warning when any such
business was towards.

Thus by degrees we began to discover Tisquantum, whose ends
were only to make himself great in the eyes of his countrymen, by
means of his nearness and favor with us; not caring who fell, so he
stood. In the general, his course was to persuade them he could lead
us to peace or war at his pleasure, and would oft threaten the
Indians, sending them word in a private manner we were intended
shortly to kill them, that thereby he might get gifts to himself, to
work their peace; insomuch as they had him in greater esteem than
many of their sachims; yea, they themselves sought to him, who
promised them peace in respect of us, yea, and protection also, so as
they would resort to him; so that whereas divers were wont to rely
on Massassowat for protection, and resort to this abode, now they
began to leave him and seek after Tisquantum. Now, though he
could not make good these his large promises, especially because of
the continued peace between Massassowat and us, he therefore
raised this false alarm; hoping, whilst things were hot in the heat of
blood, to provoke us to march into his country against him, where-
by he hoped to kindle such a flame as would not easily be quenched;
and hoping if that block were once removed, there were not other
between him and honor, which he loved as his life, and preferred
before his peace. For these and the like abuses the Governor sharply
reproved him; yet was he so necessary and profitable an instrument,
as at that time we could not miss him. But when we understood his
dealings, we certified all the Indians of our ignorance and innocen-
cy therein; assuring them, till they begun with us, they should have
no cause to fear; and if any hereafter should raise any such reports,
they should punish them as liars and seekers of their and our distur-
bance; which gave the Indians good satisfaction on all sides.

May. After this we proceeded in our voyage to the Massachusets;
1622 where we had good store of trade,[14] and (blessed be God)
     returned in safety, though driven from before our town in
great danger and extremity of weather.

At our return we found Massassowat at the Plantation; who
made his seeming just apology for all former matters of accusation,
being much offended and enraged against Tisquantum; whom the
Governor pacified as much as he could for the present. But not long
after his departure, he sent a messenger to the Governor, entreating
him to give way to the death of Tisquantum, who had so much
abused him. But the Governor answered, although he had deserved
to die, both in respect of him and us, yet for our sakes he desired he
would spare him; and the rather, because without him he knew not
well how to understand himself or any other the Indians. With this
answer the messenger returned, but came again not long after,
accompanied with divers others, demanding him from[15]
Massassowat, their master, as being one of his subjects, whom, by
our first Articles of Peace, we could not retain. Yet because he
would not willingly do it without the Governor's approbation,
offered him many beavers' skins for his consent thereto, saying that,
according to their manner, their sachim had sent his own knife, and
them therewith, to cut off his head and hands, and bring them to
him. To which the Governor answered, It was not the manner of
the English to sell men's lives at a price, but when they had deserved
justly to die, to give them their reward; and therefore refused their
beavers as a gift; but sent for Tisquantum, who, though he knew
their intent, yet offered not to fly, but came and accused
Hobbamock as the author and worker of his overthrow, yielding
himself to the Governor to be sent or not according as he thought
meet. But at the instant when our Governor was ready to deliver
him into the hands of his executioners, a boat was seen at sea to
cross before our town, and fall behind a headland[16] not far off.
Whereupon, having heard many rumors of the French, and not

May. knowing whether there were any combination between
1622 the savages and them, the Governor told the Indians he
would first know what boat that was ere he would deliver
them into their custody. But being mad with rage, and impatient at
delay, they departed in great heat.

Here let me not omit one notable, though wicked practice of this
Tisquantum; who, to the end he might possess his countrymen with
the greater fear of us, and so consequently of himself, told them we
had the plague buried in our store-house; which, at our pleasure, we
could send forth to what place or people we would, and destroy
them therewith, though we stirred not from home. Being, upon the
forenamed brabbles,[17] sent for by the Governor to this place, where
Hobbamock was and some other of us, the ground being broke in
the midst of the house, whereunder certain barrels of powder were
buried, though unknown to him, Hobbamock asked him what it
meant. To whom he readily answered, That was the place wherein
the plague was buried, whereof he formerly told him and others.
After this Hobbamock asked one of our people, whether such a
thing were, and whether we had such command of it; who answered,
No; but the God of the English had it in store, and could send it at
his pleasure to the destruction of his and our enemies.

This was, as I take it, about the end of May, 1622; at which time
our store of victuals was wholly spent, having lived long before
with a bare and short allowance. The reason was, that supply of
men, before mentioned,[18] which came so unprovided, not landing
so much as a barrel of bread or meal for their whole company, but
contrariwise received from us for their ship's store homeward.
Neither were the setters forth thereof altogether to be blamed
therein, but rather certain amongst ourselves, who were too prodi-
gal in their writing and reporting of that plenty we enjoyed.[19] But
that I may return.

This boat proved to be a shallop, that belonged to a fishing ship,
called the Sparrow, set forth by Master Thomas Weston, late mer-

June.
1622

chant and citizen of London, which brought six or seven passengers at his charge, that should before have been landed at our Plantation;[20] who also brought no more provision for the present than served the boat's gang for their return to the ship; which made her voyage at a place called Damarin's Cove,[21] near Munhiggen, some forty leagues from us northeastward; about which place there fished about thirty sail of ships, and whither myself was employed by our Governor, with orders to take up such victuals as the ships could spare; where I found kind entertainment and good respect, with a willingness to supply our wants. But being not able to spare that quantity I required, by reason of the necessity of some amongst themselves, whom they supplied before my coming, would not take any bills for the same, but did what they could freely, wishing their store had been such as they might in greater measure have expressed their own love, and supplied our necessities, for which they sorrowed, provoking one another to the utmost of their abilities; which, although it were not much amongst so many people as were at the Plantation, yet through the provident and discreet care of the governors, recovered and preserved strength till our own crop on the ground was ready.

Having dispatched there, I returned home with all speed convenient, where I found the state of the Colony much weaker than when I left it; for till now we were never without some bread, the want whereof much abated the strength and flesh of some, and swelled others. But here it may be said, if the country abound with fish and fowl in such measure as is reported, how could men undergo such measure of hardness, except through their own negligence? I answer, every thing must be expected in its proper season. No man, as one saith, will go into an orchard in the winter to gather cherries; so he that looks for fowl there in the summer, will be deceived in his expectation. The time they continue in plenty with us, is from the beginning of October to the end of March; but these extremities befell us in May and June. I confess, that as the fowl decrease, so fish

June. increase. And indeed their exceeding abundance was a
1622 great cause of increasing our wants. For though our bay and
creeks were full of bass and other fish, yet for want of fit and
strong seines and other netting, they for the most part brake
through, and carried all away before them. And though the sea were
full of cod, yet we had neither tackling nor hawsers for our shallops.
And indeed had we not been in a place, where divers sort of shellfish are, that may be taken with the hand, we must have perished,
unless God had raised some unknown or extraordinary means for
our preservation.

In the time of these straits, indeed before my going to Munhiggen,
the Indians began again to cast forth many insulting speeches, glory-
ing in our weakness, and giving out how easy it would be ere long to
cut us off. Now also Massassowat seemed to frown on us, and neither
came or sent to us as formerly. These things occasioned further
thoughts of fortification. And whereas we have a hill called the
Mount,[22] enclosed within our pale, under which our town is seated, we
resolved to erect a fort thereon; from whence a few might easily secure
the town from any assault the Indians can make, whilst the rest might
be employed as occasion served. This work was begun with great
eagerness, and with the approbation of all men, hoping that this being
once finished, and a continual guard there kept, it would utterly discourage the savages from having any hopes or thoughts of rising
against us. And though it took the greatest part of our strength from
dressing our corn, yet, life being continued, we hoped God would raise
some means in stead thereof for our further preservation.

Chapter 3

OF THE PLANTING OF MASTER WESTON'S COLONY AT WESSAGUSSET, AND OF SUNDRY EXCURSIONS AFTER CORN.

July.
1622
IN the end of June, or beginning of July, came into our harbour two ships of Master Weston's aforesaid; the one called the Charity,[1] the other the Swan; having in them some fifty or sixty men, sent over at his own charge to plant for him.[2] These we received into our town, affording them whatsoever courtesy our mean condition could afford. There the Charity, being the bigger ship, left them, having many passengers which she was to land in Virginia. In the mean time the body of them refreshed themselves at Plymouth, whilst some most fit sought out a place for them. That little store of corn we had was exceedingly wasted by the unjust and dishonest walking of these strangers; who, though they would sometimes seem to help us in our labor about our corn, yet spared not day and night to steal the same, it being then eatable and pleasant to taste, though green and unprofitable; and though they received much kindness, set light both by it and us, not sparing to requite the love we showed them, with secret backbitings, revilings, &c., the chief of them being forestalled and made against us before then came, as after appeared. Nevertheless, for their master's sake, who formerly had deserved well from us, we continued to do them whatsoever good or furtherance we could, attributing these things to the want of conscience and discretion, expecting each day when God in his providence would disburden us of them, sorrowing that their overseers were not of more ability and fitness for their places, and much fearing what would be the issue of such raw and unconscionable beginnings.

At length their coasters returned, having found in their judgment a place fit for plantation, within the bay of the Massachusets[3] at a place called by the Indians Wichaguscusset.[4] To which place the body of them went with all convenient speed, leaving still with us such as were sick and lame, by the Governor's permission, though on their parts undeserved; whom our surgeon,[5] by the help of God, recovered gratis for them, and they fetched home, as occasion served.

They had not been long from us, ere the Indians filled our ears with clamors against them, for stealing their corn, and other abuses conceived by them. At which we grieved the more, because the same men,[6] in mine own hearing, had been earnest in persuading Captain Standish, before their coming, to solicit our Governor to send some of his men to plant by them, alleging many reasons how it might be commodious for us. Be we knew no means to redress those abuses, save reproof, and advising them to better walking, as occasion served.

Aug. In the end of August, came other two ships into our har-
1622 bour. The one, as I take it, was called the Discovery, Captain Jones[7] having the command thereof; the other was that ship of Mr. Weston's, called the Sparrow, which had now made her voyage of fish, and was consorted with the other, being both bound for Virginia.[8] Of Captain Jones we furnished ourselves of such provisions as we most needed, and he could best spare; who, as he used us kindly, so made us pay largely for the things we had. And had not the Almighty, in his all-ordering providence, directed him to us, it would have gone worse with us than ever it had been, or after was; for as we had now but small store of corn for the year following, so, for want of supply, we were worn out of all manner of trucking-stuff, not having any means left to help ourselves by trade; but, through God's good mercy towards us, he had wherewith, and did supply our wants on that kind competently.[9]

Oct. In the end of September, or beginning of October, Mr.
1622 Weston's biggest ship, called the Charity, returned for England, and left their colony sufficiently victualled, as some of most credit amongst them reported. The lesser, called the Swan, remained with his colony, for their further help. At which

time they desired to join in partnership with us, to trade for corn; to which our Governor and his Assistant[10] agreed, upon such equal conditions, as were drawn and confirmed between them and us. The chief places aimed at were to the southward of Cape Cod; and the more, because Tisquantum, whose peace before this time was wrought with Massassowat, undertook to discover unto us that supposed, and still hoped, passage within the shoals.

Both colonies being thus agreed, and their companies fitted and joined together, we resolved to set forward, but were oft crossed in our purposes. As first Master Richard Greene, brother-in-law to master Weston, who from him had a charge in the oversight and government of his colony, died suddenly at our Plantation, to whom we gave burial befitting his place, in the best manner we could. Afterward, having further order to proceed by letter from their other Governor at the Massachusets, twice Captain Standish set forth with them, but were driven in again by cross and violent winds; himself the second time being sick of a violent fever. By reason whereof (our own wants being like to be now greater than formerly, partly because we were enforced to neglect our corn and spend much time in fortification, but especially because such havock was made of that little we had, through the unjust and dishonest carriage of those people, before mentioned, at our first entertainment of them,) our Governor in his
Nov. own person supplied the Captain's place; and, in the
1622 month of November, again set forth, having Tisquantum for his interpreter and pilot; who affirmed he had twice passed within the shoals of Cape Cod, both with English and French. Nevertheless they went so far with him, as the master of the ship saw no hope of passage; but being, as he thought, in danger, bare up, and according to Tisquantum's directions, made for a harbour not far from them, at a place called Manamoycke; which they found, and sounding it with their shallop, found the channel, though but narrow and crooked; where at length they harboured

Nov. the ship. Here they perceived that the tide set in and out
1622 with more violence at some other place more southerly,[11]
        which they had not seen nor could discover, by reason of
the violence of the season all the time of their abode there. Some
judged the entrance thereof might be beyond the shoals; but there
is no certainty thereof as yet known.

That night the Governor, accompanied with others, having
Tisquantum for his interpreter, went ashore. At first, the inhabitants played least in sight, because none of our people had ever
been there before; but understanding the ends of their coming, at
length came to them, welcoming our Governor according to their
savage manner; refreshing them very well with store of venison and
other victuals, which they brought them in great abundance;
promising to trade with them, with a seeming gladness of the occasion. Yet their joy was mixed with much jealousy, as appeared by
their after practices; for at first they were loth their dwellings
should be known; but when they saw our Governor's resolution to
stay on the shore all night, they brought him to their houses, having first conveyed all their stuff to a remote place, not far from the
same; which one of our men, walking forth occasionally, espied.
Whereupon, on the sudden, neither it nor they could be found; and
so many times after, upon conceived occasions, they would be all
gone, bag and baggage. But being afterwards, by Tisquantum's
means better persuaded, they left their jealousy, and traded with
them; where they got eight hogsheads of corn and beans, though
the people were but few. This gave our Governor and the company
good encouragement; Tisquantum being still confident in the passage, and the inhabitants affirming they had seen ships of good burthen pass within the shoals aforesaid.

But here, though they had determined to make a second essay,
yet God had otherways disposed; who struck Tisquantum with sickness, insomuch as he there died;[12] which crossed their southward
trading, and the more, because the master's sufficiency was much

doubted, and the season very tempestuous, and not fit to go upon discovery, having no guide to direct them.

From thence they departed; and the wind being fair for the Massachusets, went thither, and the rather, because the savages, upon our motion, had planted much corn for us, which they promised not long before that time. When they came thither, they found a great sickness to be amongst the Indians, not unlike the plague, if not the same. They renewed their complaints to our Governor, against the other plantation seated by them, for their injurious walking. But indeed the trade both for furs and corn was overthrown in that place, they giving as much for a quart of corn as we used to do for a beaver's skin; so that little good could be there done.

From thence they returned into the bottom of the bay of Cape Cod, to a place called Nauset; where the sachim[13] used the Governor very kindly, and where they bought eight or ten hogsheads of corn and beans; also at a place called Mattachiest,[14] where they had like kind entertainment and corn also. During the time of their trade in these places, there were so great and violent storms, as the ship was much endangered, and our shallop cast away; so that they had now no means to carry the corn aboard that they had bought, the ship riding by their report well near two leagues from the same, her own boat being small, and so leaky, (having no carpenter with them,) as they durst scarce fetch wood or water in her. Hereupon the Governor caused the corn to be made in a round stack, and bought mats, and cut sedge, to cover it; and gave charge to the Indians not to meddle with it, promising him that dwelt next to it a reward, if he would keep vermin also from it; which he undertook, and the sachim promised to make good. In the mean time, according to the Governor's request, the sachim sent men to seek the shallop; which they found buried almost in sand at a high water mark, having many things remaining in her, but unserviceable for the present; whereof the Governor gave the sachim special charge,

Nov. that it should not be further broken, promising ere long to
1622 fetch both it and the corn; assuring them, if neither were
diminished, he would take it as a sign of their honest and
true friendship, which they so much made show of; but if they were,
they should certainly smart for their unjust and dishonest dealing,
and further make good whatsoever they had so taken. So he did likewise at Mattachiest, and took leave of them, being resolved to leave
the ship and take his journey home by land with our own company,
sending word to the ship that they should take their first opportunity to go for Plymouth, where he determined, by the permission of
God, to meet them. And having procured a guide, it being no less
than fifty miles to our Plantation,[15] set forward, receiving all respect
that could be from the Indians in his journey; and came safely home,
though weary and surbated;[16] whither some three days after the
ship[17] also came.

The corn being divided, which they had got, Master Weston's
company went to their own plantation; it being further agreed, that
they should return with all convenient speed, and bring their carpenter, that they might fetch the rest of the corn, and save the shallop.

Jan. At their return, Captain Standish, being recovered and in
1623 health, took another shallop, and went with them to the
corn, which they found in safety as they left it. Also they
mended the other shallop, and got all their corn aboard the ship.
This was in January, as I take it, it being very cold and stormy; insomuch as, (the harbour being none of the best,) they were constrained to cut both the shallops from the ship's stern; and so lost
them both a second time. But the storm being over, and seeking out,
they found them both, not having received any great hurt.

Whilst they were at Nauset, having occasion to lie on the shore,
laying their shallop in a creek[18] not far from them, an Indian came
into the same, and stole certain beads, scissors, and other trifles, out
of the same; which, when the Captain missed, he took certain of
his company with him and went to the sachim, telling him what

Jan. 1623 had happened, and requiring the same again, or the party that stole them, (who was known to certain of the Indians,) or else he would revenge it on them before his departure; and so took leave for that night, being late, refusing whatsoever kindness they offered. On the morrow the sachim came to their rendezvous, accompanied with many men, in a stately manner, who saluted[19] the Captain in this wise. He thrust out his tongue, that one might see the root thereof, and therewith licked his hand from the wrist to the finger's end, withal bowing the knee, striving to imitate the English gesture, being instructed therein formerly by Tisquantum. His men did the like, but in so rude and savage a manner, as our men could scarce forbear to break out in open laughter. After salutation, he delivered the beads and other things to the Captain, saying he had much beaten the party for doing it; causing the women to make bread, and bring them, according to their desire; seeming to be very sorry for the fact, but glad to be reconciled. So they departed and came home in safety; where the corn was equally divided, as before.

After this the Governor went to two other inland towns, with another company, and bought corn likewise of them. The one is called Namasket, the other Manomet.[20] That from Namasket was brought home partly by Indian women;[21] but a great sickness arising amongst them, our own men were enforced to fetch home the rest. That at Manomet the Governor left in the sachim's custody.

This town lieth from us south, well near twenty miles, and stands upon a fresh river, which runneth into the bay of Nano-higganset,[22] and cannot be less than sixty miles from thence. It will bear a boat of eight or ten tons to this place. Hither the Dutch or French, or both, use to come. It is from hence to the bay of Cape Cod, about eight miles;[23] out of which bay it floweth into a creek some six miles, almost direct towards the town. The heads of the river and this creek are not far distant. This river yieldeth, thus high, oysters,[24] muscles, clams,[25] and other shellfish; one in shape like a

Jan.
1623
bean,[26] another like a clam; both good meat, and great abundance at all times; besides it aboundeth with divers sorts of fresh fish in their seasons.[27]

The Governor, or sachim, of this place was called Canacum;[28] who had formerly, as well as many others, yea all with whom as yet we had to do, acknowledged themselves the subjects of our sovereign lord, the King. This sachim used the Governor very kindly; and it seemed was of good respect and authority amongst the Indians. For whilst the Governor was there, within night, in bitter weather, came two men from Manamoick, before spoken of; and having set aside their bows and quivers, according to their manner, sat down by the fire, and took a pipe of tobacco, not using any words in that time, nor any other to them, but all remained silent, expecting when they would speak. At length they looked toward Canacum; and one of them made a short speech, and delivered a present to him from his sachim, which was a basket of tobacco and many beads, which the other received thankfully. After which he made a long speech to him; the contents hereof was related to us by Hobbamock (who then accompanied the Governor for his guide,) to be as followeth. It happened that two of their men fell out, as they were in game, (for they use gaming as much as any where, and will play away all, even their skin from their backs,[29] yea their wives' skins also, though it may be they are many miles distant from them, as myself have seen,) and growing to great heat, the one killed the other. The actor of this fact was a *powah*,[30] one of special note amongst them, and such an one as they could not well miss; yet another people greater than themselves threatened them with war, if they would not put him to death. The party offending was in hold; neither would their sachim do one way or other till their return, resting upon him for advice and furtherance in so weighty a matter. After this there was silence a short time. At length, men gave their judgment what they thought best. Amongst others, he asked Hobbamock what he thought; who answered, He was but a stranger to them; but thought it was better that one should die than many, since he had deserved it, and the rest were innocent. Whereupon he passed the sentence of death upon him.

Feb. Not long after, having no great quantity of corn left,
1623 Captain Standish went again with a shallop to Mattachiest, meeting also with the like extremity of weather, both of wind, snow, and frost; insomuch as they were frozen in the harbour, the first night they entered the same. Here they pretended their wonted love, and spared them a good quantity of corn to confirm the same. Strangers also came to this place, pretending only to see him and his company, whom they never saw before that time, but intending to join with the rest to kill them, as after appeared. But being forced through extremity to lodge in their houses, which they much pressed, God possessed the heart of the Captain with just jealousy, giving strait command, that as one part of his company slept, the rest should wake, declaring some things to them which he understood, whereof he could make no good construction.

Some of the Indians, spying a fit opportunity, stole some beads also from him; which he no sooner perceived, having not above six men with him, drew them all from the boat, and set them on their guard about the sachim's house, where the most of the people were; threatening to fall upon them without further delay, if they would not forthwith restore them; signifying to the sachim especially, and so to them all, that as he would not offer the least injury, so he would not receive any at their hands, which should escape without punishment or due satisfaction. Hereupon the sachim bestirred him to find out the party; which, when he had done, caused him to return them again to the shallop, and came to the Captain, desiring him to search whether they were not about the boat; who, suspecting their knavery, sent one, who found them lying openly upon the boat's cuddy. Yet to appease his anger, they brought corn afresh to trade; insomuch as he laded his shallop, and so departed. This accident so daunted their courage, as they durst not attempt any thing against him. So that, through the good mercy and providence of God, they returned in safety. At this place the Indians get abundance of bass both summer and winter; for it being now February, they abounded with them.

Mar. In the beginning of March, having refreshed himself, he
1623 took a shallop, and went to Manomet, to fetch home that which the Governor had formerly bought,[31] hoping also to get more from them; but was deceived in his expectation, not finding that entertainment he found elsewhere, and the Governor had there received. The reason whereof, and of the treachery intended in the place before spoken of, was not then known unto us, but afterwards; wherein may be observed the abundant mercies of God, working with his providence for our good. Captain Standish being now far from the boat, and not above two or three of our men with him, and as many with the shallop, was not long at Canacum, the sachim's house, but in came two of the Massachuset men. The chief of them was called Wituwamat, a notable insulting villain, one who had formerly imbrued his hands in the blood of English and French, and had oft boasted of his own valour, and derided their weakness, especially because, as he said, they died crying, making sour faces, more like children than men.

This villain took a dagger from about his neck, which he had gotten of Master Weston's people, and presented it to the sachim; and after made a long speech in an audacious manner, framing it in such sort, as the Captain, though he be the best linguist amongst us,[32] could not gather any thing from it. The end of it was afterwards discovered to be as followeth. The Massacheuseuks had formerly concluded to ruinate Master Weston's colony; and thought themselves, being about thirty or forty men, strong enough to execute the same. Yet they durst not attempt it, till such time as they had gathered more strength to themselves, to make their party good against us at Plymouth; concluding, that if we remained, though they had

Mar. no other arguments to use against us, yet we would never
1623 leave the death of our countrymen unrevenged; and therefore their safety could not be without the overthrow of
both plantations. To this end they had formerly solicited this
sachim, as also the other, called Ianough,[33] at Mattachiest, and many
others, to assist them, and now again came to prosecute the same;
and since there was so fair an opportunity offered by the Captain's
presence, they thought best to make sure [of] him and his company.

After this his message was delivered, his entertainment much
exceeded the Captain's; insomuch as he scorned at their behaviour,
and told them of it. After which they would have persuaded him,
because the weather was cold, to have sent to the boat for the rest of
his company; but he would not, desiring, according to promise, that
the corn might be carried down, and he would content the women[34]
for their labor; which they did. At the same time there was a lusty
Indian of Paomet,[35] or Cape Cod, then present, who had ever
demeaned himself well toward us, being in his general carriage very
affable, courteous, and loving, especially towards the Captain. This
savage was now entered into confederacy with the rest; yet, to avoid
suspicion, made many signs of his continued affections, and would
needs bestow a kettle of some six or seven gallons on him, and
would not accept of any thing in lieu thereof, saying he was rich and
could afford to bestow such favors on his friends whom he loved.
Also he would freely help to carry some of the corn, affirming he had
never done the like in his life before; and the wind being bad, would
needs lodge with him at their rendezvous, having indeed undertak-
en to kill him before they parted; which done, they intended to fall
upon the rest.

The night proved exceeding cold; insomuch as the Captain
could not take any rest, but either walked, or turned himself to and
fro at the fire. This the other observed, and asked wherefore he did
not sleep as at other times; who answered, He knew not well, but
had no desire at all to rest. So that he then missed his opportunity.

Mar. The wind serving on the next day, they returned home,
<u>1623</u> accompanied with the other Indian; who used many argu-
ments to persuade them to go to Paomet, where himself
had much corn, and many other, the most whereof he would procure for us, seeming to sorrow for our wants. Once the Captain put
forth with him, and was forced back by contrary wind; which wind
serving for the Massachuset, was fitted to go thither. But on a sudden it altered again.

Chapter 4

WINSLOW'S SECOND JOURNEY
TO PACKANOKICK, TO VISIT
MASSASOIT IN HIS SICKNESS.

Mar.
1623

DURING the time that the Captain was at Manomet, news came to Plymouth that Massassowat was like to die, and that at the same time there was a Dutch ship driven so high on the shore by stress of weather, right before his dwelling, that till the tides increased, she could not be got off. Now it being a commendable manner of the Indians, when any, especially of note, are dangerously sick, for all that profess friendship to them to visit them in their extremity,[1] either in their persons, or else to send some acceptable persons to them; therefore it was thought meet, being a good and warrantable action, that as we had ever professed friendship, so we should now maintain the same, by observing this their laudable custom; and the rather, because we desired to have some conference with the Dutch, not knowing when we should have so fit an opportunity. To that end, myself having formerly been there, and understanding in some measure the Dutch tongue, the Governor again laid this service upon myself, and fitted me with some cordials to administer to him; having one Master John Hamden,[2] a gentleman of London, who then wintered with us, and desired much to see the country, for my consort, and Hobbamock for our guide. So we set forward, and lodged the first night at Namasket, where we had friendly entertainment.

The next day, about one of the clock, we came to a ferry[3] in Conbatant's country, where, upon discharge of my piece, divers Indians came to us from a house not far off. There they told us that Massassowat was dead, and that day buried; and that the Dutch would be gone before we could get thither, having hove off their ship already. This news struck us blank, but especially Hobbamock,

★ *Mar.* who desired we might return with all speed. I told him I
　1623 would first think of it. Considering now, that he being
　　　　 dead, Conbatant⁴ was the most like to succeed him, and
that we were not above three miles from Mattapuyst,⁵ his dwelling-
place, although he were but a hollowhearted friend toward us, I
thought no time so fit as this to enter into more friendly terms with
him, and the rest of the sachims thereabout; hoping, through the
blessing of God, it would be a means, in that unsettled state, to settle their affections towards us; and though it were somewhat dangerous, in respect of our personal safety, because myself and
Hobbamock had been employed upon a service against him, which
he might now fitly revenge; yet esteeming it the best means, leaving
the event to God in his mercy, I resolved to put it in practice, if
Master Hamden and Hobbamock durst attempt it with me; whom I
found willing to that or any other course might tend to the general
good. So we went towards Mattapuyst.

In the way, Hobbamock, manifesting a troubled spirit, brake
forth into these speeches: *Neen womasu sagimus, neen womasu sagimus,* &c. "My loving sachim, my loving sachim! Many have I
known, but never any like thee." And turning him to me, said,
whilst I lived, I should never see his like amongst the Indians; saying, he was no liar, he was not bloody and cruel, like other Indians;
in anger and passion he was soon reclaimed; easy to be reconciled
towards such as had offended him; ruled by reason in such measure
as he would not scorn the advice of mean men; and that he gov-
erned his men better with few strokes, than others did with many;
truly loving where he loved; yea, he feared we had not a faithful
friend left among the Indians; showing, how he ofttimes restrained
their malice, &c., continuing a long speech, with such signs of
lamentation and unfeigned sorrow, as it would have made the hard-
est heart relent.

At length we came to Mattapuyst, and went to the *sachimo coma-
co,*⁶ for so they call the sachim's place, though they call an ordinary

Mar. house *witeo*;[7] but Conbatant, the sachim, was not at home,
1623 but at Puckanokick, which was some five or six miles off.

The *squasachim*, for so they call the sachim's wife, gave us friendly entertainment. Here we inquired again concerning Massassowat; they thought him dead, but knew no certainty. Whereupon I hired one to go with all expedition to Puckanokick, that we might know the certainty thereof, and withal to acquaint Conbatant with our there being. About half an hour before sunsetting the messenger returned, and told us that he was not yet dead, though there was no hope we should find him living. Upon this we were much revived, and set forward with all speed, though it was late within night ere we got thither. About two from the clock that afternoon, the Dutchmen departed; so that in that respect our journey was frustrate.

When we came thither, we found the house so full of men, as we could scarce get in, though they used their best diligence to make way for us. There were they in the midst of their charms for him, making such a hellish noise, as it distempered us that were well, and therefore unlike to ease him that was sick.[8] About him were six or eight women, who chafed his arms, legs, and thighs, to keep heat in him. When they had made an end of their charming, one told him that his friends, the English, were come to see him. Having understanding left, but his sight was wholly gone, he asked, Who was come? They told him Winsnow, for they cannot pronounce the letter *l*, but ordinarily *n* in place thereof.[9] He desired to speak with me. When I came to him, and they told him of it, he put forth his hand to me, which I took. Then he said twice, though very inwardly, *Keen Winsnow?* which is to say, "Art thou Winslow?" I answered, *Ahhe*, that is, Yes. Then he doubled these words; *Matta neen wonckanet namen, Winsnow!* that is to say, "O Winslow, I shall never see thee again."

Then I called Hobbamock, and desired him to tell Massassowat, that the Governor, hearing of his sickness, was sorry for the same; and

Mar. though, by reason of many businesses, he could not come
1623 himself, yet he sent me with such things for him as he
thought most likely to do him good in this his extremity;[10]
and whereof if he pleased to take, I would presently give him; which
he desired; and having a confection of many comfortable conserves,
&c., on the point of my knife I gave him some, which I could scarce
get through his teeth. When it was dissolved in his mouth, he swallowed the juice of it, whereat those that were about him much
rejoiced, saying he had not swallowed any thing in two days before.
Then I desired to see his mouth, which was exceedingly furred, and
his tongue swelled in such a manner, as it was not possible for him to
eat such meat as they had, his passage being stopped up. Then I
washed his mouth, and scraped his tongue, and got abundance of cor-
ruption out of the same. After which I gave him more of the confection, which he swallowed with more readiness. Then he desiring to
drink, I dissolved some of it in water, and gave him thereof. Within
half an hour this wrought a great alteration in him, in the eyes of all
that beheld him. Presently after his sight began to come to him,
which gave him and us good encouragement. In the mean time I
inquired how he slept, and when he went to stool. They said he slept
not in two days before, and had not had a stool in five. Then I gave
him more, and told him of a mishap we had by the way, in breaking a
bottle of drink, which the Governor also sent him, saying if he would
send any of his men to Patuxet, I would send for more of the same;
also for chickens to make him broth, and for other things, which I
knew were good for him; and would stay the return of his messenger,
if he desired. This he took marvellous kindly, and appointed some,
who were ready to go by two of the clock in the morning; against
which time I made ready a letter, declaring therein our good success,
the state of his body, &c., desiring to send me such things as I sent for,
and such physic as the surgeon durst administer to him.

He requested me, that the day following, I would take my piece,
and kill him some fowl, and make him some English pottage, such

Mar. as he had eaten at Plymouth; which I promised. After, his
1623 stomach coming to him, I must needs make him some
without fowl, before I went abroad, which somewhat troubled me, being unaccustomed and unacquainted in such businesses,
especially having nothing to make it comfortable, my consort being
as ignorant as myself; but being we must do somewhat, I caused a
woman to bruise some corn, and take the flour from it, and set over
the grit, or broken corn, in a pipkin, for they have earthen pots of all
sizes. When the day broke, we went out, it being now March, to seek
herbs, but could not find any but strawberry leaves, of which I gathered a handful, and put into the same; and because I had nothing to
relish it, I went forth again, and pulled up a sassafras root, and sliced
a piece thereof, and boiled it, till it had a good relish, and then took
it out again. The broth being boiled, I strained it through my hand-
kerchief, and gave him at least a pint, which he drank, and liked it
very well. After this his sight mended more and more; also he had
three moderate stools, and took some rest; insomuch as we with
admiration blessed God for giving his blessing to such raw and ignorant means, making no doubt of his recovery, himself and all of them
acknowledging us the instruments of his preservation.

That morning he caused me to spend in going from one to
another amongst those that were sick in the town, requesting me to
wash their mouths also, and give to each of them some of the same
I gave him, saying they were good folk. This pains I took with willingness, though it were much offensive to me, not being accus-
tomed with such poisonous savours. After dinner he desired me to
get him a goose or duck, and make him some pottage therewith,
with as much speed as I could. So I took a man with me, and made
a shot at a couple of ducks, some six score paces off, and killed one,
at which he wondered. So we returned forthwith and dressed it,
making more broth therewith, which he much desired. Never did I
see a man so low brought, recover in that measure in so short a
time. The fowl being extraordinary fat, I told Hobbamock I must

Mar. take off the top thereof, saying it would make him very
1623 sick again if he did eat it. This he acquainted Massassowat
therewith, who would not be persuaded to it, though I
pressed it very much, showing the strength thereof, and the weakness of his stomach, which could not possibly bear it.
Notwithstanding, he made a gross meal of it, and ate as much as
would well have satisfied a man in health. About an hour after he
began to be very sick, and straining very much, cast up the broth
again; and in overstraining himself, began to bleed at the nose, and
so continued the space of four hours. Then they all wished he had
been ruled, concluding now he would die, which we much feared
also. They asked me what I thought of him. I answered, his case was
desperate, yet it might be it would save his life; for if it ceased in
time, he would forthwith sleep and take rest, which was the principal thing he wanted. Not long after his blood stayed, and he slept
at least six or eight hours. When he awaked, I washed his face, and
bathed and suppled his beard and nose with a linen cloth. But on a
sudden he chopped his nose in the water, and drew up some therein, and sent it forth again with such violence, as he began to bleed
afresh. Then they thought there was no hope; but we perceived it
was but the tenderness of his nostril, and therefore told them I
thought it would stay presently, as indeed it did.

The messengers were now returned; but finding his stomach
come to him, he would not have the chickens killed, but kept them
for breed. Neither durst we give him any physic, which was then
sent, because his body was so much altered since our instructions;
neither saw we any need, not doubting now of his recovery, if he
were careful. Many, whilst we were there, came to see him; some, by
their report, from a place not less than an hundred miles. To all that
came one of his chief men related the manner of his sickness, how
near he was spent, how amongst others his friends the English came
to see him, and how suddenly they recovered him to this strength
they saw, he being now able to sit upright of himself.

Mar. The day before our coming, another sachim being there,
1623 told him that now he might see how hollow-hearted the
English were, saying if we had been such friends in deed, as
we were in show, we would have visited him in this his sickness,
using many arguments to withdraw his affections, and to persuade
him to give way to some things against us, which were motioned to
him not long before. But upon his recovery, he brake forth into
these speeches: Now I see the English are my friends and love me;
and whilst I live, I will never forget this kindness they have showed
me. Whilst we were there, our entertainment exceeded all other
strangers'. Divers other things were worthy the noting; but I fear I
have been too tedious.

At our coming away, he called Hobbamock to him, and privately (none hearing, save two or three other of his *pnieses*,[11] who
are of his council) revealed the plot of the Massacheuseucks, before
spoken of, against Master Weston's colony, and so against us; saying
that the people of Nauset, Paomet, Succonet,[12] Mattachiest,
Manomet, Agowaywam,[13] and the isle of Capawack,[14] were joined
with them; himself also in his sickness was earnestly solicited, but
he would neither join therein, nor give way to any of his.
Therefore, as we respected the lives of our countrymen, and our
own after safety, he advised us to kill the men of Massachuset, who
were the authors of this intended mischief. And whereas we were
wont to say, we would not strike a stroke till they first began; if, said
he, upon this intelligence, they make that answer, tell them, when
their countrymen at Wichaguscusset are killed, they being not able
to defend themselves, that then it will be too late to recover their
lives; nay, through the multitude of adversaries, they shall with
great difficulty preserve their own; and therefore he counselled
without delay to take away the principals, and then the plot would
cease. With this he charged him thoroughly to acquaint me by the
way, that I might inform the Governor thereof, at my first coming
home. Being fitted for our return, we took our leave of him; who

Mar. returned many thanks to our Governor, and also to our-
1623 selves for our labor and love; the like did all that were
      about him. So we departed.

That night, through the earnest request of Conbatant, who till
now remained at Sawaams, or Puckanokick, we lodged with him at
Mattapuyst. By the way I had much conference with him, so likewise at his house, he being a notable politician, yet full of merry jests
and squibs, and never better pleased than when the like are returned
again upon him. Amongst other things he asked me, if in case he
were thus dangerously sick, as Massassowat had been, and should
send word thereof to Patuxet for *maskiet*,[15] that is, physic, whether
then Mr. Governor would send it; and if he would, whether I would
come therewith to him. To both which I answered, Yea; whereat he
gave me many joyful thanks. After that, being at his house, he
demanded further, how we durst, being but two, come so far into the
country. I answered, where was true love, there was no fear; and my
heart was so upright towards them, that for mine own part I was fearless to come amongst them. But, said he, if your love be such, and it
bring forth such fruits, how cometh it to pass, that when we come to
Patuxet, you stand upon your guard, with the mouths of your pieces
presented towards us? Whereupon I answered, it was the most honorable and respective entertainment we could give them; it being an
order amongst us so to receive our best respected friends; and as it
was used on the land, so the ships observed it also at sea, which
Hobbamock knew and had seen observed. But shaking the head, he
answered, that he liked not such salutations.

Further, observing us to crave a blessing on our meat before we
did eat, and after to give thanks for the same, he asked us, what was
the meaning of that ordinary custom. Hereupon I took occasion to
tell them of God's works of creation and preservation, of his laws
and ordinances, especially of the ten commandments; all which
they hearkened unto with great attention, and like well of; only the
seventh commandment they excepted against, thinking there were

Mar. many inconveniences in it, that a man should be tied to
1623 one woman; about which we reasoned a good time. Also I
told them, that whatsoever good things we had, we
received from God, as the author and giver thereof; and therefore
craved his blessing upon that we had, and were about to eat, that it
might nourish and strengthen our bodies; and having eaten sufficient, being satisfied therewith, we again returned thanks to the
same our God, for that our refreshing, &c. This all of them concluded to be very well; and said, they believed almost all the same
things, and that the same power that we called God, they called
Kiehtan.[16] Much profitable conference was occasioned hereby, which
would be too tedious to relate, yet was no less delightful to them,
than comfortable to us. Here we remained only that night, but
never had better entertainment amongst any of them.

The day following, in our journey, Hobbamock told me of the
private conference he had with Massassowat, and how he charged
him perfectly to acquaint me therewith, as I showed before; which
having done, he used many arguments himself to move us thereunto. That night we lodged at Namasket; and the day following, about
the mid-way between it and home, we met two Indians, who told us,
that Captain Standish was that day gone to the Massachusets. But
contrary winds again drove him back; so that we found him at
home; where the Indian of Paomet still was, being very importunate
that the Captain should take the first opportunity of a fair wind to
go with him. But their secret and villainous purposes being, through
God's mercy, now made known, the Governor caused Captain
Standish to send him away, without any distaste or manifestation of
anger, that we might the better effect and bring to pass that which
should be thought most necessary.

Chapter 5

OF STANDISH'S EXPEDITION AGAINST THE
INDIANS OF WESSAGUSSET, AND THE BREAKING
UP OF WESTON'S COLONY AT THAT PLACE.

Feb.
1623

BEFORE this journey we heard many complaints, both by the Indians, and some others of best desert amongst Master Weston's colony, how exceedingly their company abased themselves by indirect means, to get victuals from the Indians, who dwelt not far from them, fetching them wood and water, &c. and all for a meal's meat; whereas, in the mean time, they might with diligence have gotten enough to have served them three or four times. Other by night brake the earth, and robbed the Indians' store; for which they had been publicly stocked and whipped, and yet was there small amendment. This was about the end of February; at which time they had spent all their bread and corn, not leaving any for seed, neither would the Indians lend or sell them any more upon any terms. Hereupon they had thoughts to take it by violence; and to that spiked up every entrance into their town, being well impaled, save one, with a full resolution to proceed. But some more honestly minded advised John Sanders, their overseer, first to write to Plymouth; and if the Governor advised him thereunto, he might the better do it. This course was well liked, and an Indian was sent with all speed with a letter to our Governor, the contents whereof were to this effect; that being in great want, and their people daily falling down, he intended to go to Munhiggen, where was a plantation of Sir Ferdinando Gorges, to buy bread from the ships that came thither a fishing, with the first opportunity of wind; but knew not how the colony would be preserved till his return. He had used all means both to buy and borrow of Indians, whom he knew to be stored, and he thought maliciously withheld it, and therefore was resolved to

Mar. take it by violence, and only waited the return of the mes-
1623 senger, which he desired should be hastened, craving his
advice therein, promising also to make restitution afterward. The Governor, upon the receipt hereof, asked the messenger
what store of corn they had, as if he had intended to buy of them;
who answered, very little more than that they reserved for seed,
having already spared all they could.

Forthwith the Governor and his Assistant sent for many of us to
advise with them herein; who, after serious consideration, no way
approving of this intended course, the Governor answered his letter,
and caused many of us to set our hands thereto; the contents whereof were to this purpose. We altogether disliked their intendment, as
being against the law of God and nature, showing how it would cross
the worthy ends and proceedings of the King's Majesty, and his honorable Council for this place, both in respect of the peaceable
enlarging of his Majesty's dominions, and also of the propagation of
the knowledge and law of God, and the glad tidings of salvation,
which we and they were bound to seek, and were not to use such
means as would breed a distaste in the savages against our persons
and professions, assuring them their master would incur much blame
hereby, neither could they answer the same. For our own parts, our
case was almost the same with theirs, having but a small quantity of
corn left, and were enforced to live on ground-nuts, clams, muscles,
and such other things as naturally the country afforded, and which
did and would maintain strength, and were easy to be gotten; all
which things they had in great abundance, yea, oysters[1] also, which
we wanted; and therefore necessity could not be said to constrain
them thereunto. Moreover, that they should consider, if they proceeded therein, all they could so get would maintain them but a
small time, and then they must perforce seek their food abroad;
which, having made the Indians their enemies, would be very difficult for them, and therefore much better to begin a little the sooner, and so continue their peace; upon which course they might with

Mar. good conscience desire and expect the blessing of God;
1623 whereas on the contrary they could not.

Also that they should consider their own weakness, being
most swelled, and diseased in their bodies, and therefore the more
unlikely to make their party good against them, and that they
should not expect help from us in that or any the like unlawful
actions. Lastly, that howsoever some of them might escape, yet the
principal agents should expect no better than the gallows, whensoever any special officer should be sent over by his Majesty, or his
Council for New England, which we expected, and who would
undoubtedly call them to account for the same. These were the
contents of our answer, which was directed to their whole colony.
Another particular letter our Governor sent to John Sanders,
showing how dangerous it would be for him above all others, being
he was their leader and commander; and therefore in friendly manner advised him to desist.

With these letters we dispatched the messenger; upon the receipt
whereof they altered their determination, resolving to shift as they
could, till the return of John Sanders from Munhiggen; who first
coming to Plymouth, notwithstanding our own necessities, the
Governor spared him some corn, to carry them to Munhiggen. But
not having sufficient for the ship's store, he took a shallop, and
leaving others with instructions to oversee things till his return, set
forward about the end of February; so that he knew not of this conspiracy of the Indians before his going. Neither was it known to any
of us till our return from Sawaams, or Puckanokick; at which time
also another sachim, called Wassapinewat, brother to Obtakiest, the
sachim of the Massachusets, who had formerly smarted for partaking
with Conbatant, and fearing the like again, to purge himself,
revealed the same thing.

The three and twentieth of March being now come, which is a
yearly court day, the Governor, having a double testimony, and
many circumstances agreeing with the truth thereof, not being[2] to

Mar. undertake war without the consent of the body of the com-
1623 pany, made known the same in public court, offering it to
the consideration of the company, it being high time to
come to resolution, how sudden soever it seemed to them, fearing it
would be put in execution before we could give any intelligence
thereof. This business was no less troublesome than grievous, and
the more, because it is so ordinary in these times for men to measure
things by the events thereof; but especially for that we knew no
means to deliver our countrymen and preserve ourselves, than by
returning their malicious and cruel purposes upon their own heads,
and causing them to fall into the same pit they had digged for others; though it much grieved us to shed the blood of those whose
good we ever intended and aimed at, as a principal in all our proceedings. But in the end we came to this public conclusion, that
because it was a matter of such weight as every man was not of sufficiency to judge, nor fitness to know, because of many other
Indians, which daily, as occasion serveth, converse with us; therefore the Governor, his Assistant, and the Captain, should take such
to themselves as they thought most meet, and conclude thereof.
Which done, we came to this conclusion, that Captain Standish
should take so many men, as he thought sufficient to make his party
good against all the Indians in the Massachuset bay; and because,
(as all men know that have to do with them in that kind,) it is
impossible to deal with them upon open defiance, but to take them
in such traps as they lay for others, therefore he should pretend
trade, as at other times; but first go to the English, and acquaint
them with the plot, and the end of his own coming; that comparing
it with their carriages towards them, he might the better judge of
the certainty of it, and more fitly take opportunity to revenge the
same; but should forbear, if it were possible, till such time as he
could make sure [of] Wituwamat, that bloody and bold villain
before spoken of; whose head he had order to bring with him, that
he might be a warning and terror to all of that disposition.

24 Upon this Captain Standish made choice of eight men,
Mar. and would not take more, because he would prevent jeal-
1623 ousy, knowing their guilty consciences would soon be provoked thereunto. But on the next day, before he could go, came
one[3] of Mr. Weston's company by land unto us, with his pack at his
back, who made a pitiful narration of their lamentable and weak
estate, and of the Indians' carriages, whose boldness increased
abundantly; insomuch as the victuals they got, they would take it
out of their pots, and eat before their faces; yea, if in any thing they
gainsaid them, they were ready to hold a knife at their breasts; that
to give them content, since John Sanders went to Munhiggen,
they had hanged[4] one of them that stole their corn, and yet they
regarded it not; that another of their company was turned salvage;
that their people had most forsaken the town, and made their rendezvous where they got their victuals, because they would not take
pains to bring it home; that they had sold their clothes for corn, and
were ready to starve both with cold and hunger also, because they
could not endure to get victuals by reason of their nakedness; and
that they were dispersed into three companies, scarce having any
powder and shot left. What would be the event of these things he
said he much feared; and therefore not daring to stay any longer
among them, though he knew not the way, yet adventured to come
to us; partly to make known their weak and dangerous estate, as he
conceived, and partly to desire he might there remain till things
were better settled at the other plantation. As this relation was
grievous to us, so it gave us good encouragement to proceed in our
intendments, for which Captain Standish was now fitted; and the
wind coming fair, the next day set forth for the Massachusets.

The Indians at the Massachusets missed this man; and suspecting his coming to us, as we conceive, sent one after him, and gave
out there that he would never come to Patuxet, but that some
wolves or bears would eat him. But we know, both by our own experience, and the reports of others, that though they find a man

25 sleeping, yet so soon as there is life discerned, they fear and
Mar. shun him. This Indian missed him but very little; and
1623 missing him, passed by the town and went to Manomet;
whom we hoped to take at his return, as afterward we did. Now was
our fort made fit for service, and some ordnance mounted; and
though it may seem long work, it being ten months since it begun,
yet we must note, that where so great a work is begun with such
small means, a little time cannot bring [it] to perfection. Beside,
those works which tend to the preservation of man, the enemy of
mankind will hinder, what in him lieth, sometimes blinding the
judgment, and causing reasonable men to reason against their own
safety; as amongst us divers seeing the work prove tedious, would
have dissuaded from proceeding, flattering themselves with peace
and security, and accounting it rather a work of superfluity and
vainglory, than simple necessity. But God, whose providence hath
waked, and, as I may say, watched for us whilst we slept, having
determined to preserve us from these intended treacheries,
undoubtedly ordained this as a special means to advantage us and
discourage our adversaries, and therefore so stirred up the hearts of
the governors and other forward instruments, as the work was just
made serviceable against this needful and dangerous time, though
we ignorant of the same.

But that I may proceed, the Indian last mentioned, in his return
from Manomet, came through the town, pretending still friendship
and in love to see us; but as formerly others, so his end was to see
whether we continued still in health and strength, or fell into
weakness, like their neighbours; which they hoped and looked for,
(though God in mercy provided better for us,) and he knew would
be glad tidings to his countrymen. But here the Governor stayed
him; and sending for him to the fort, there gave the guard charge of
him as their prisoner; where he told him he must be contented to
remain till the return of Captain Standish from the Massachusets.
So he was locked in a chain to a staple in the court of guard, and

Mar. there kept. Thus was our fort hanselled,[5] this being the
1623 first day, as I take it, that ever any watch was there kept.

The Captain, being now come to the Massachusets, went
first to the ship; but found neither man, or so much as a dog therein. Upon the discharge of a musket, the master and some others of
the plantation showed themselves, who were on the shore gath-
ering ground-nuts, and getting other food. After salutation,
Captain Standish asked them how they durst so leave the ship,
and live in such security; who answered, like men senseless of
their own misery, they feared not the Indians, but lived and suf-
fered them to lodge with them, not having sword or gun, or need-
ing the same. To which the Captain answered, if there were no
cause, he was the gladder. But, upon further inquiry, understanding that those in whom John Sanders had reposed most special
confidence, and left in his stead to govern the rest, were at the
plantation, thither he went; and, to be brief, made known the
Indians' purpose, and the end of his own coming, as also, (which
formerly I omitted,) that if afterward they durst not there stay, it
was the intendment of the governors and people of Plymouth
there to receive them, till they could be better provided; but if
they conceived of any other course, that might be more likely for
their good, that himself should further them therein to the utter-
most of his power. These men, comparing other circumstances
with that they now heard, answered, they could expect no better;
and it was God's mercy that they were not killed before his coming; desiring therefore that he would neglect no opportunity to
proceed. Hereupon he advised them to secrecy, yet withal to send
special command to one third of their company, that were farthest
off, to come home, and there enjoin them on pain of death to
keep the town, himself allowing them a pint of Indian corn to a
man for a day, though that store he had was spared out of our seed.
The weather proving very wet and stormy, it was the longer before
he could do any thing.

Mar. In the mean time an Indian came to him, and brought
1623 some furs, but rather to gather what he could from the
Captain, than coming then for trade; and though the
Captain carried things as smoothly as possibly he could, yet at his
return he reported he saw by his eyes that he was angry in his heart;
and therefore began to suspect themselves discovered. This caused
one Pecksuot, who was a *pniese*,[6] being a man of a notable spirit, to
come to Hobbamock, who was then with them, and told him, he
understood that the Captain was come to kill himself and the rest of
the salvages there. "Tell him," said he, "we know it, but fear him not,
neither will we shun him; but let him begin when he dare, he shall
not take us at unawares." Many times after, divers of them severally,
or few together, came to the plantation to him; where they would
whet and sharpen the points of their knives before his face, and use
many other insulting gestures and speeches. Amongst the rest
Wituwamat bragged of the excellency of his knife. On the end of the
handle there was pictured a woman's face; "but," said he, "I have
another at home, wherewith I have killed both French and English,
and that hath a man's face on it; and by and by these two must
marry." Further he said of that knife he there had, *Hinnaim namen,
hinnaim michen, matta cuts;* that is to say, By and by it should see, and
by and by it should eat, but not speak. Also Pecksuot, being a man
of greater stature than the Captain,[7] told him, though he were a
great captain, yet he was but a little man; and, said he, though I be
no sachim, yet I am a man of great strength and courage. These
things the Captain observed, yet bare with patience for the present.

On the next day, seeing he could not get many of them together
at once, and this Pecksuot and Wituwamat both together, with
another man, and a youth of some eighteen years of age, which was
brother to Wituwamat, and, villain-like, trod in his steps, daily
putting many tricks upon the weaker sort of men, and having about
as many of his own company in a room with them, gave the word to
his men, and the door being fast shut, began himself with Pecksuot,

Mar. and snatching his own knife from his neck, though with
1623 much struggling, killed him therewith, the point whereof
he had made as sharp as a needle, and ground the back also
to an edge. Wituwamat and the other man the rest killed, and took
the youth, whom the Captain caused to be hanged. But it is incredible how many wounds these two pineses received before they died,
not making any fearful noise, but catching at their weapons and
striving to the last. Hobbamock stood by all this time as a spectator,
and meddled not, observing how our men demeaned themselves in
this action. All being here ended, smiling, he brake forth into these
speeches to the Captain: "Yesterday Pecksuot, bragging of his own
strength and stature, said, though you were a great captain, yet you
were but a little man; but to-day I see you are big enough to lay him
on the ground." But to proceed; there being some women at the
same time, Captain Standish left them in the custody of Mr.
Weston's people at the town, and sent word to another company,
that had intelligence of things, to kill those Indian men that were
amongst them. These killed two more. Himself also with some of his
own men went to another place, where they killed another; and
through the negligence of one man, an Indian escaped, who discovered and crossed their proceedings.[8]

Not long before this execution, three of Mr. Weston's men,
which more regarded their bellies than any command or commander, having formerly fared well with the Indians for making them
canoes, went again to the sachim to offer their service, and had
entertainment. The first night they came thither, within night, late
came a messenger with all speed, and delivered a sad and short message. Whereupon all the men gathered together, put on their boots
and breeches, trussed up themselves, and took their bows and arrows
and went forth, telling them they went a hunting, and that at their
return they should have venison enough. Being now gone, one
being more ancient and wise than the rest, calling former things to
mind, especially the Captain's presence, and the strait charge that

Mar. on pain of death none should go a musket shot from the
1623 plantation, and comparing this sudden departure of theirs
therewith, began to dislike and wish himself at home again,
which was further off than divers other dwelt. Hereupon he moved
his fellows to return, but could not persuade them. So there being
none but women left, and the other that was turned salvage, about
midnight came away, forsaking the paths, lest he should be pursued;
and by this means saved his life.

Captain Standish took the one half of his men, and one or two
of Mr. Weston's, and Hobbamock, still seeking to make spoil of
them and theirs. At length they espied a file of Indians, which
made towards them amain; and there being a small advantage in
the ground, by reason of a hill near them, both companies strove for
it. Captain Standish got it; whereupon they retreated, and took
each man his tree, letting fly their arrows amain, especially at himself and Hobbamock. Whereupon Hobbamock cast off his coat,
and being a known pinese, (theirs being now killed,) chased them
so fast, as our people were not able to hold way with him; insomuch
as our men could have but one certain mark, and then but the arm
and half face of a notable villain, as he drew[9] at Captain Standish;
who together with another both discharged at once at him, and
brake his arm; whereupon they fled into a swamp. When they were
in the thicket, they parleyed, but to small purpose, getting nothing
but foul language. So our Captain dared the sachim to come out and
fight like a man, showing how base and woman-like he was in
tonguing it as he did; but he refused, and fled. So the Captain
returned to the plantation; where he released the women, and
would not take their beaver coats from them, nor suffer the least dis-
courtesy to be offered them.

Now were Mr. Weston's people resolved to leave their plantation, and go for Munhiggen, hoping to get passage and return[10]
with the fishing ships. The Captain told them, that for his own
part he durst there live with fewer men than they were; yet since

Mar. they were otherways minded, according to his order from
1623 the governors and people of Plymouth, he would help
them with corn competent for their provision by the way;
which he did, scarce leaving himself more than brought them
home. Some of them disliked the choice of the body to go to
Munhiggen, and therefore desiring to go with him to Plymouth, he
took them into the shallop; and seeing them set sail, and clear of
the Massachuset bay,[11] he took leave and returned to Plymouth;
whither he came in safety, blessed be God! and brought the head
of Wituwamat with him.

Among the rest, there was an Indian youth, that was ever of a
courteous and loving disposition towards us. He, notwithstanding
the death of his countrymen, came to the Captain without fear, saying, his good conscience and love towards us imboldened him so to
do. This youth confessed, that the Indians intended to kill Mr.
Weston's people, and not to delay any longer than till they had two
more canoes or boats, which Mr. Weston's men would have finished
by this time, having made them three already, had not the Captain
prevented them; and the end of stay for those boats was to take their
ship therewith.

Now was the Captain returned and received with joy, the head
being brought to the fort, and there set up.[12] The governors and captains with divers others went up the same further, to examine the
prisoner, who looked piteously on the head. Being asked whether he
knew it, he answered, Yea. Then he confessed the plot, and that all
the people provoked Obtakiest, their sachim, thereunto, being
drawn to it by their importunity. Five there were, he said, that prosecuted it with more eagerness than the rest. The two principal were
killed, being Pecksuot and Wituwamat, whose head was there; the
other three were powahs, being yet living, and known unto us,
though one of them was wounded, as aforesaid. For himself, he
would not acknowledge that he had any hand therein, begging
earnestly for his life, saying he was not a Massachuset man, but as a

Mar. stranger lived with them. Hobbamock also gave a good
<u>1623</u> report of him, and besought for him; but was bribed so to
do. Nevertheless, that we might show mercy as well as
extremity, the Governor released him, and the rather, because we
desired he might carry a message to Obtakiest, his master. No sooner were the irons from his legs, but he would have been gone; but the
Governor bid him stay, and fear not, for he should receive no hurt;
and by Hobbamock commanded him to deliver this message to his
master: That for our parts it never entered into our hearts to take
such a course with them, till their own treachery enforced us thereunto, and therefore they might thank themselves for their own
overthrow; yet since he had begun, if again by any the like courses
he did provoke him, his country should not hold him; for he would
never suffer him or his to rest in peace, till he had utterly consumed
them; and therefore should take this as a warning; further, that he
should send to Patuxet the three Englishmen he had, and not kill
them; also that he should not spoil the pale and houses at
Wichaguscusset; and that this messenger should either bring the
English, or an answer, or both; promising his safe return.

This message was delivered, and the party would have returned
with [an] answer, but was at first dissuaded by them, whom afterwards they would, but could not persuade to come to us. At length,
though long, a woman came and told us that Obtakiest was sorry
that the English were killed, before he heard from the Governor;
otherwise he would have sent them. Also she said, he would fain
make his peace again with us, but none of his men durst come to
treat about it, having forsaken his dwelling, and daily removed
from place to place, expecting when we would take further
vengeance on him.

Concerning those other people, that intended to join the
Massacheuseuks against us, though we never went against any of
them; yet this sudden and unexpected execution, together with the
just judgment of God upon their guilty consciences, hath so terrified

Mar. and amazed them, as in like manner they forsook their
1623 houses, running to and fro like men distracted, living in
swamps and other desert places, and so brought manifold
diseases amongst themselves, whereof very many are dead; as
Canacum, the sachim of Manomet, Aspinet, the sachim of Nauset,
and Ianough, sachim of Mattachiest. This sachim in his life, in the
midst of these distractions, said the God of the English was offended
with them, and would destroy them in his anger; and certainly it is
strange to hear how many of late have, and still daily die amongst
them. Neither is there any likelihood it will easily cease; because
through fear they set little or no corn, which is the staff of life, and
without which they cannot long preserve health and strength. From
one of these places a boat was sent with presents to the Governor,
hoping thereby to work their peace; but the boat was cast away, and
three of the persons drowned, not far from our Plantation. Only one
escaped, who durst not come to us, but returned; so as none of them
dare come amongst us.

I fear I have been too tedious both in this and other things. Yet
when I considered how necessary a thing it is that the truth and
grounds of this action especially should be made known, and the
several dispositions of that dissolved colony, whose reports undoubtedly will be as various, I could not but enlarge myself where I
thought to be most brief. Neither durst I be too brief, lest I should
eclipse and rob God of that honor, glory, and praise, which
belongeth to him for preserving us from falling when we were at the
pit's brim, and yet feared nor knew not that we were in danger.

Chapter 6

OF THE FIRST ALLOTMENT OF LANDS,
AND THE DISTRESSED STATE
OF THE COLONY.

April.
1623

THE month of April being now come, on all hands we began to prepare for corn. And because there was no corn left before this time, save that was preserved for seed, being also hopeless of relief by supply, we thought best to leave off all other works, and prosecute that as most necessary. And because there was no[1] small hope of doing good, in that common course of labor that formerly we were in; for that the governors, that followed men to their labors, had nothing to give men for their necessities, and therefore could not so well exercise that command over them therein, as formerly they had done; especially considering that self-love wherewith every man, in a measure more or less, loveth and preferreth his own good before his neighbour's, and also the base disposition of some drones, that, as at other times, so now especially would be most burdensome to the rest; it was therefore thought best that every man should use the best diligence he could for his own preservation, both in respect of the time present, and to prepare his own corn for the year following; and bring in a competent portion for the maintenance of public officers, fishermen, &c., which could not be freed from their calling without greater inconveniences. This course was to continue till harvest, and then the governors to gather in the appointed portion, for the maintenance of themselves and such others as necessity constrained to exempt from this condition. Only if occasion served, upon any special service they might employ such as they thought most fit to execute the same, during this appointed time, and at the end thereof all men to be employed by them in such service as they thought most necessary for the general good. And because there is great difference in the ground, that therefore a set

April.
1623 quantity should be set down for a person, and each man to have his fall by lot,[2] as being most just and equal, and against which no man could except.

At a general meeting of the company, many courses were propounded, but this approved and followed, as being the most likely for the present and future good of the company; and therefore before this month began to prepare our ground against seed-time.

In the midst of April we began to set, the weather being then seasonable, which much encouraged us, giving us good hopes of after plenty. The setting season is good till the latter end of May. But it pleased God, for our further chastisement, to send a great drought, insomuch as in six weeks after the latter setting there scarce fell any

July.
1623 rain; so that the stalk of that was first set began to send forth the ear, before it came to half growth, and that which was later not like to yield any at all, both blade and stalk hanging the head, and changing the color in such manner, as we judged it utterly dead. Our beans also ran not up according to their wonted manner, but stood at a stay, many being parched away, as though they had been scorched before the fire. Now were our hopes overthrown, and we discouraged, our joy being turned into mourning.[3]

To add also to this sorrowful estate in which we were, we heard of a supply that was sent unto us many months since, which having two repulses before, was a third time in company of another ship three hundred leagues at sea, and now in three months time heard no further of her; only the signs of a wreck were seen on the coast, which could not be judged to be any other than the same.[4] So that at once God seemed to deprive us of all future hopes. The most courageous were now discouraged, because God, which hitherto had been our only shield and supporter, now seemed in his anger to arm himself against us. And who can withstand the fierceness of his wrath?

These and the like considerations moved not only every good man privately to enter into examination with his own estate

July. between God and his conscience, and so to humiliation
1623 before him, but also more solemnly to humble ourselves
together before the Lord by fasting and prayer. To that end
a day was appointed by public authority, and set apart from all other
employments; hoping that the same God, which had stirred us up
hereunto, would be moved hereby in mercy to look down upon us,
and grant the request of our dejected souls, if our continuance there
might any way stand with his glory and our good. But Oh the mercy
of our God! who was as ready to hear, as we to ask; for though in the
morning, when we assembled together, the heavens were as clear,
and the drought as like to continue as ever it was, yet, (our exercise
continuing some eight or nine hours,) before our departure, the
weather was overcast, the clouds gathered together on all sides, and
on the next morning distilled such soft, sweet, and moderate show-
ers of rain, continuing some fourteen days, and mixed with such seasonable weather, as it was hard to say whether our withered corn or
drooping affections were most quickened or revived; such was the
bounty and goodness of our God. Of this the Indians, by means of
Hobbamock,[5] took notice; who being then in the town, and this
exercise in the midst of the week, said, It was but three days since
Sunday; and therefore demanded of a boy, what was the reason
thereof. Which when he knew, and saw what effects followed there-
upon, he and all of them admired the goodness of our God towards
us, that wrought so great a change in so short a time; showing the
difference between their conjuration, and our invocation on the
name of God for rain; theirs being mixed with such storms and tempests, as sometimes, instead of doing them good, it layeth the corn
flat on the ground, to their prejudice; but ours in so gentle and seasonable a manner, as they never observed the like.

At the same time Captain Standish, being formerly employed by
the Governor to buy provisions for the refreshing of the Colony,
returned with the same, accompanied with one Mr. David Tomson,[6]
a Scotchman, who also that spring began a plantation twenty-five

July. 1623 leagues northeast from us, near Smith's isles,[7] at a place called Pascatoquack, where he liketh well. Now also heard we of the third repulse that our supply had,[8] of their safe, though dangerous, return into England, and of their preparation to come to us. So that having these many signs of God's favor and acceptation, we thought it would be great ingratitude, if secretly we should smother up the same, or content ourselves with private thanksgiving for that, which by private prayer could not be obtained. And therefore another solemn day was set apart and appointed for that end; wherein we returned glory, honor, and praise, with all thankfulness, to our good God, which dealt so graciously with us; whose name for these and all other his mercies towards his church, and chosen ones, by them be blessed and praised, now and evermore. Amen.

In the latter end of July, and the beginning of August, came two ships with supply unto us; who brought all their passengers,[9] except one, in health, who recovered in short time; who, also, notwithstanding all our wants and hardship, blessed be God! found not any one sick person amongst us at the Plantation. The bigger ship, called the Anne,[10] was hired, and there again freighted back;[11] from whence we set sail the 10th of September. The lesser, called the LITTLE JAMES,[12] was built for the company at their charge.[13] She was now also fitted for trade and discovery to the southward of Cape Cod, and almost ready to set sail; whom I pray God to bless in her good and lawful proceedings.

Chapter 7

OF THE MANNERS, CUSTOMS, RELIGIOUS OPINIONS AND CEREMONIES OF THE INDIANS.

1623

THUS have I made a true and full narration of the state of our Plantation, and such things as were most remarkable therein since December, 1621. If I have omitted any thing, it is either through weakness of memory, or because I judged it not material. I confess my style rude, and unskilfulness in the task I undertook; being urged thereunto by opportunity, which I knew to be wanting in others, and but for which I would not have undertaken the same. Yet as it is rude, so it is plain, and therefore the easier to be understood; wherein others may see that which we are bound to acknowledge, viz. that if ever any people in these later ages were upheld by the providence of God after a more special manner than others, then we; and therefore are the more bound to celebrate the memory of his goodness with everlasting thankfulness. For in these forenamed straits, such was our state, as in the morning we had often our food to seek for the day, and yet performed the duties of our callings, I mean other daily labors, to provide for after time; and though at some times in some seasons at noon I have seen men stagger by reason of faintness for want of food, yet ere night, by the good providence and blessing of God, we have enjoyed such plenty as though the windows of heaven had been opened unto us. How few, weak, and raw were we at our first beginning, and there settling, and in the midst of barbarous enemies! Yet God wrought our peace for us. How often have we been at the pit's brim, and in danger to be swallowed up, yea, not knowing till afterward that we were in peril! And yet God preserved us; yea, and from how many that we yet know not of, He that knoweth all things can best tell. So that when I seriously consider of things, I cannot but think that God hath a purpose to give that land as an inheritance to our nation, and great pity it were that it should long lie in so deso-

_____ late a state, considering it agreeth so well with the consti-
1623 tution of our bodies, being both fertile, and so temperate
for heat and cold, as in that respect one can scarce distinguish New England from Old.

A few things I thought meet to add hereunto, which I have
observed amongst the Indians, both touching their religion and
sundry other customs amongst them. And first, whereas myself and
others, in former letters, (which came to the press against my will
and knowledge,) wrote that the Indians about us are a people without any religion, or knowledge of any God, therein I erred, though
we could then gather no better; for as they conceive of many divine
powers, so of one, whom they call *Kiehtan*,[1] to be the principal and
maker of all the rest, and to be made by none. He, they say, created
the heavens, earth, sea and all creatures contained therein; also
that he made one man and one woman, of whom they and we and
all mankind came;[2] but how they became so far dispersed, that
know they not. At first, they say, there was no sachim or king, but
Kiehtan, who dwelleth above in the heavens, whither all good
men go when they die, to see their friends, and have their fill of all
things. This his habitation lieth far westward in the heavens, they
say; thither the bad men go also, and knock at his door, but he bids
them *quatchet*, that is to say, walk abroad, for there is no place for
such; so that they wander in restless want and penury.[3] Never man
saw this Kiehtan; only old men tell of him, and bid them tell their
children, yea to charge them to teach their posterities the same,
and lay the like charge upon them. This power they acknowledge
to be good; and when they would obtain any great matter, meet
together and cry unto him; and so likewise for plenty, victory, &c.
sing, dance, feast, give thanks, and hang up garlands and other
things in memory of the same.

Another power they worship, whom they call *Hobbamock*, and
to the northward of us, *Hobbamoqui*;[4] this, as far as we can conceive,
is the devil. Him they call upon to cure their wounds and diseases.

When they are curable, he persuades them he sends the same for some conceived anger against them; but upon their calling upon him, can and doth help them; but when they are mortal and not curable in nature, then he persuades them Kiehtan is angry, and sends them, whom none can cure; insomuch as in that respect only they somewhat doubt whether he be simply good, and therefore in sickness never call upon him. This Hobbamock appears in sundry forms unto them, as in the shape of a man, a deer, a fawn, an eagle, &c. but most ordinarily a snake. He appears not to all, but the chiefest and most judicious amongst them; though all of them strive to attain to that hellish height of honor. He appeareth most ordinary and is most conversant with three sorts of people. One, I confess I neither know by name nor office directly; of these they have few, but esteem highly of them, and think that no weapon can kill them; another they call by the name of *powah*; and the third *pniese*.

The office and duty of the powah is to be exercised principally in calling upon the devil, and curing diseases of the sick or wounded. The common people join with him in the exercise of invocation, but do but only assent, or as we term it, say Amen to that he saith; yet sometime break out into a short musical note with him. The powah is eager and free in speech, fierce in countenance, and joineth many antic and laborious gestures with the same, over the party diseased.[5] If the party be wounded, he will also seem to suck the wound; but if they be curable, (as they say,) he toucheth it not, but *askooke*, that is, the snake, or *wobsacuck*, that is, the eagle, sitteth on his shoulder, and licks the same. This none see but the powah, who tells them he doth it himself. If the party be otherwise diseased, it is accounted sufficient if in any shape he but come into the house, taking it for an undoubted sign of recovery.

And as in former ages Apollo had his temple at Delphos, and Diana at Ephesus, so have I heard them call upon some as if they had their residence in some certain places, or because they appeared in

_____
1623 those forms in the same. In the powah's speech, he
promiseth to sacrifice many skins of beasts, kettles, hatchets, beads, knives, and other the best things they have to
the fiend, if he will come to help the party diseased; but whether
they perform it, I know not. The other practices I have seen, being
necessarily called sometimes to be with their sick, and have used the
best arguments I could to make them understand against the same.
They have told me I should see the devil at those times come to the
party; but I assured myself and them of the contrary, which so
proved; yea, themselves have confessed they never saw him when
any of us were present. In desperate and extraordinary hard travail
in child-birth, when the party cannot be delivered by the ordinary
means, they send for this powah; though ordinarily their travail is
not so extreme as in our parts of the world, they being of a more
hardy nature; for on the third day after child-birth, I have seen the
mother with the infant, upon a small occasion, in cold weather, in a
boat upon the sea.

Many sacrifices the Indians use, and in some cases kill children.
It seemeth they are various in their religious worship in a little distance, and grow more and more cold in their worship to Kiehtan;
saying, in their memory he was much more called upon. The
Nanohiggansets exceed in their blind devotion, and have a great
spacious house, wherein only some few (that are, as we may term
them, priests) come. Thither, at certain known times, resort all their
people, and offer almost all the riches they have to their gods, as kettles, skins, hatchets, beads, knives, &c., all which are cast by the
priests into a great fire that they make in the midst of the house, and
there consumed to ashes. To this offering every man bringeth freely;
and the more he is known to bring, hath the better esteem of all
men. This the other Indians about us approve of as good, and wish
their sachims would appoint the like; and because the plague hath
not reigned at Nanohigganset as at other places about them, they
attribute to this custom there used.

_____ The pnieses are men of great courage and wisdom, and to
1623   those also the devil appeareth more familiarly than to others, and as we conceive, maketh covenant with them to
preserve them from death by wounds with arrows, knives, hatchets,
&c. or at least both themselves and especially the people think
themselves to be freed from the same. And though, against their
battles, all of them by painting disfigure themselves, yet they are
known by their courage and boldness, by reason whereof one of
them will chase almost an hundred men; for they account it death
for whomsoever stand in their way. These are highly esteemed of all
sorts of people, and are of the sachim's council, without whom they
will not war, or undertake any weighty business.[6] In war their
sachims, for their more safety, go in the midst of them. They are
commonly men of the greatest stature and strength, and such as will
endure most hardness, and yet are more discreet, courteous and
humane in their carriages than any amongst them, scorning theft,
lying, and the like base dealings, and stand as much upon their rep-
utation as any men. And to the end they may have store of these,
they train up the most forward and likeliest boys, from their child-
hood, in great hardness, and make them abstain from dainty meat,
observing divers orders prescribed, to the end that when they are of
age, the devil may appear to them; causing to drink the juice of sen-
try[7] and other bitter herbs, till they cast, which they must disgorge
into the platter, and drink again and again, till at length through
extraordinary oppressing of nature, it will seem to be all blood; and
this the boys will do with eagerness at the first, and so continue till
by reason of faintness, they can scarce stand on their legs, and then
must go forth into the cold. Also they beat their shins with sticks,
and cause them to run through bushes, stumps and brambles, to
make them hardy and acceptable to the devil, that in time he may
appear unto them.

Their sachims cannot be all called kings, but only some few of
them, to whom the rest resort for protection, and pay homage unto

them;[8] neither may they war without their knowledge and approbation; yet to be commanded by the greater, as occasion serveth. Of this sort is Massassowat, our friend, and Conanacus, of Nanohigganset, our supposed enemy. Every sachim taketh care for the widow and fatherless, also for such as are aged and any way maimed, if their friends be dead, or not able to provide for them. A sachim will not take any to wife, but such an one as is equal to him in birth; otherwise, they say, their seed would in time become ignoble; and though they have many other wives, yet are they no other than concubines or servants, and yield a kind of obedience to the principal, who ordereth the family and them in it. The like their men observe also, and will adhere to the first during their lives; but put away the other at their pleasure. This government is successive, and not by choice. If the father die before the son or daughter be of age, then the child is committed to the protection and tuition of some one amongst them, who ruleth in his stead till he be of age; but when that is, I know not.

Every sachim knoweth how far the bounds and limits of his own country extendeth; and that is his own proper inheritance. Out of that, if any of his men desire land to set their corn, he giveth them as much as they can use, and sets them their bounds. In this circuit whosoever hunteth, if they kill any venison, bring him his fee; which is the fore parts of the same, if it be killed on the land, but if in the water, then the skin thereof. The great sachims or kings know their own bounds or limits of land, as well as the rest. All travellers or strangers for the most part lodge at the sachim's. When they come, they tell them how long they will stay, and to what place they go; during which time they receive entertainment, according to their persons, but want not. Once a year the pnieses use to provoke the people to bestow much corn on the sachim. To that end, they appoint a certain time and place, near the sachim's dwelling, where the people bring many baskets of corn, and make a great stack thereof. There the pnieses stand ready to give thanks

_____
1623
to the people, on the sachim's behalf; and after acquaint the sachim therewith, who fetcheth the same, and is no less thankful, bestowing many gifts on them.

When any are visited with sickness, their friends resort unto them for their comfort, and continue with them ofttimes till their death or recovery.[9] If they die, they stay a certain time to mourn for them. Night and morning they perform this duty, many days after the burial, in a most doleful manner, insomuch as though it be ordinary and the note musical, which they take one from another and all together, yet it will draw tears from their eyes, and almost from ours also.[10] But if they recover, then because their sickness was chargeable, they send corn and other gifts unto them, at a certain appointed time, whereat they feast and dance, which they call *commoco*. When they bury the dead, they sow up the corpse in a mat, and so put it in the earth. If the party be a sachim, they cover him with many curious mats, and bury all his riches with him, and enclose the grave with a pale. If it be a child, the father will also put his own most special jewels and ornaments in the earth with it; also will cut his hair, and disfigure himself very much, in token of sorrow. If it be the man or woman of the house, they will pull down the mats, and leave the frame standing, and bury them in or near the same, and either remove their dwelling or give over housekeeping.

The men employ themselves wholly in hunting, and other exercises of the bow, except at some times they take some pains in fishing. The women live a most slavish life; they carry all their burdens,[11] set and dress their corn, gather it in, seek out for much of their food, beat and make ready the corn to eat, and have all household care lying upon them.

The younger sort reverence the elder, and do all mean offices, whilst they are together, although they be strangers. Boys and girls may not wear their hair like men and women, but are distinguished thereby.

_____ A man is not accounted a man till he do some notable act,
1623 or show forth such courage and resolution as becometh his
        place. The men take much tobacco; but for boys so to do,
they account it odious.

All their names are significant and variable; for when they come to the state of men and women, they alter them according to their deeds or dispositions.

When a maid is taken in marriage, she first cutteth her hair, and after weareth a covering on her head, till her hair be grown out. Their women are diversely disposed; some as modest, as they will scarce talk one with another in the company of men, being very chaste also; yet other some light, lascivious and wanton. If a woman have a bad husband, or cannot affect him, and there be war or opposition between that and any other people, she will run away from him to the contrary party, and there live; where they never come unwelcome, for where are most women, there is greatest plenty.

When a woman hath her monthly terms, she separateth herself from all other company, and liveth certain days in a house alone; after which, she washeth herself, and all that she hath touched or used, and is again received to her husband's bed or family. For adultery, the husband will beat his wife and put her away, if he please. Some common strumpets there are, as well as in other places; but they are such as either never married, or widows, or put away for adultery; for no man will keep such an one to wife.

In matters of unjust and dishonest dealing, the sachim examineth and punisheth the same. In case of thefts, for the first offence, he is disgracefully rebuked; for the second, beaten by the sachim with a cudgel on the naked back; for the third, he is beaten with many strokes, and hath his nose slit upwards, that thereby all men may both know and shun him. If any man kill another, he must likewise die for the same. The sachim not only passes the sentence upon malefactors,[12] but executeth the same with his own

_____
1623

hands, if the party be then present; if not, sendeth his own knife, in case of death, in the hands of others to perform the same.[13] But if the offender be to receive other punishment, he will not receive the same but from the sachim himself; before whom, being naked, he kneeleth, and will not offer to run away, though he beat him never so much, it being a greater disparagement for a many to cry during the time of his correction, than is his offence and punishment.

As for their apparel, they wear breeches and stockings in one, like some Irish, which is made of deer skins, and have shoes of the same leather. They wear also a deer's skin loose about them, like a cloak, which they will turn to the weather side. In this habit they travel; but when they are at home, or come to their journey's end, presently they pull off their breeches, stockings and shoes, wring out the water, if they be wet, and dry them, and rub or chafe the same. Though these be off, yet have they another small garment that covereth their secrets. The men wear also, when they go abroad in cold weather, an otter or fox skin on their right arm, but only their bracer on the left. Women, and all of that sex, wear strings about their legs, which the men never do.

The people are very ingenious and observative; they keep account of time by the moon, and winters or summers; they know divers of the stars by name; in particular they know the north star, and call it *maske*, which is to say, the bear;[14] also they have many names for the winds. They will guess very well at the wind and weather beforehand, by observations in the heavens. They report also, that some of them can cause the wind to blow in what part they list—can raise storms and tempests,[15] which they usually do when they intend the death or destruction of other people, that by reason of the unseasonable weather, they may take advantage of their enemies in their houses. At such times they perform their greatest exploits, and in such seasons, when they are at enmity with any, they keep more careful watch than at other times.

_____   As for the language, it is very copious, large, and difficult.
_1623_   As yet we cannot attain to any great measure thereof; but
           can understand them, and explain ourselves to their
understanding, by the help of those that daily converse with us.
And though there be difference in a hundred miles' distance of
place, both in language and manners, yet not so much but that
they very well understand each other.[16] And thus much of their
lives and manners.

Instead of records and chronicles, they take this course. Where
any remarkable act is done, in memory of it, either in the place, or
by some pathway near adjoining, they make a round hole in the
ground, about a foot deep, and as much over; which when others
passing by behold, they inquire the cause and occasion of the same,
which being once known, they are careful to acquaint all men, as
occasion serveth, therewith; and lest such holes should be filled or
grown up by any accident, as men pass by, they will oft renew the
same; by which means many things of great antiquity are fresh in
memory. So that as a man travelleth, if he can understand his guide,
his journey will be the less tedious, by reason of the many historical
discourses [which] will be related unto him.

Chapter 8

OF THE SITUATION, CLIMATE, SOIL, AND PRODUCTIONS OF NEW ENGLAND.

1623

IN all this, it may be said, I have neither praised nor dispraised the country; and since I lived so long therein, my judgment thereof will give no less satisfaction to them that know me, than the relation of our proceedings. To which I answer, that as in one, so of the other, I will speak as sparingly as I can, yet will make known what I conceive thereof.

And first for that continent, on which we are, called New England, although it hath ever been conceived by the English to be a part of the main land adjoining the Virginia, yet by relation of the Indians it should appear to be otherwise; for they affirm confidently that it is an island, and that either the Dutch or French pass through from sea to sea between us and Virginia, and drive a great trade in the same. The name of the inlet of the sea they call Mohegon, which I take to be the same which we call Hudson's river, up which Master Hudson went many leagues, and for want of means (as I hear) left it undiscovered.[1] For confirmation of this their opinion, is thus much; though Virginia be not above a hundred and fifty leagues from us, yet they never heard of Powhatan, or knew that any English were planted in his country, save only by us and Tisquantum, who went in an English ship thither; and therefore it is the more probable, because the water is not passable for them, who are very adventurous in their boats.

Then for the temperature of the air, in almost three years' experience I can scarce distinguish New England from Old England, in respect of heat and cold, frost, snow, rain, winds, &c. Some object, because our Plantation lieth in the latitude of 42°, it must needs be much hotter. I confess I cannot give the reason of the contrary; only experience teacheth us, that if it do exceed England, it is so little as must require better judgments to discern it. And for the winter, I

_____ rather think (if there be difference) it is both sharper and
1623 longer in New England than Old; and yet the want of those
        comforts in the one, which I have enjoyed in the other,
may deceive my judgment also. But in my best observation, comparing our own condition with the Relations of other parts of
America, I cannot conceive of any to agree better with the consti-
tution of the English, not being oppressed with extremity of heat,
nor nipped by biting cold; by which means, blessed be God, we
enjoy our health, notwithstanding those difficulties we have undergone, in such a measure as would have been admired if we had lived
in England with the like means. The day is two hours longer than
here, when it is at the shortest, and as much shorter there, when it
is at the longest.

The soil is variable, in some places mould, in some clay, others, a
mixed sand, &c. The chiefest grain is the Indian mays, or Guinea
wheat. The seed time beginneth in [the] midst of April, and contin-
ueth good till the midst of May. Our harvest beginneth with
September. This corn increaseth in great measure, but is inferior in
quantity to the same in Virginia; the reason I conceive is because
Virginia is far hotter than it is with us, it requiring great heat to ripen.
But whereas it is objected against New England, that corn will not
grow there except the ground be manured with fish, I answer, that
where men set with fish, (as with us,) it is more easy so to do than to
clear ground, and set without some five or six years, and so begin
anew, as in Virginia and elsewhere. Not but that in some places,
where they cannot be taken with ease in such abundance, the
Indians set four years together without, and have as good corn or better than we have that set with them; though indeed I think if we had
cattle to till the ground, it would be more profitable and better agree-
able to the soil to sow wheat, rye, barley, pease and oats, than to set
mays, which our Indians call *ewachim*; for we have had experience
that they like and thrive well; and the other will not be procured
without good labor and diligence, especially at seed-time, when it

must also be watched by night, to keep the wolves from the fish, till it be rotten, which will be in fourteen days. Yet men agreeing together, and taking their turns, it is not much.

Much might be spoken of the benefit that may come to such as shall here plant, by trade with the Indians for furs, if men take a right course for obtaining the same; for I dare presume, upon that small experience I have had, to affirm that the English, Dutch and French return yearly many thousand pounds profit by trade only from that island on which we are seated.

Tobacco may be there planted, but not with that profit as in some other places; neither were it profitable there to follow it, though the increase were equal, because fish is a better and richer commodity, and more necessary, which may be and are there had in as great abundance as in any other part of the world; witness the west-country merchants of England, which return incredible gains yearly from thence. And if they can so do, which here buy their salt at a great charge, and transport more company to make their voyage than will sail their ships, what may the planters expect when once they are seated, and make the most of their salt there, and employ themselves at least eight months in fishing; whereas the other fish but four, and have their ship lie dead in the harbour all the time, whereas such shipping as belong to plantations may take freight of passengers or cattle thither, and have their lading provided against they come? I confess we have come so far short of the means to raise such returns, as with great difficulty we have preserved our lives; insomuch as when I look back upon our condition, and weak means to preserve the same, I rather admire at God's mercy and providence in our preservation, than that no greater things have been effected by us. But though our beginning have been thus raw, small and difficult, as thou hast seen, yet the same God that hath hitherto led us through the former, I hope will raise means to accomplish the latter. Not that we altogether, or principally, propound profit to be the main end of that we have undertaken, but the glory of God, and the

<u>1623</u> honor of our country, in the enlarging of his Majesty's dominions. Yet wanting outward means to set things in that forwardness we desire, and to further the latter by the former, I thought meet to offer both to consideration, hoping that where religion and profit jump together (which is rare) in so honorable an action, it will encourage every honest man, either in person or purse, to set forward the same, or at leastwise to commend the welfare thereof in his daily prayers to the blessing of the blessed God.

I will not again speak of the abundance of fowl, store of venison, and variety of fish, in their seasons, which might encourage many to go in their persons. Only I advise all such beforehand to consider, that as they hear of countries that abound with the good creatures of God, so means must be used for the taking of every one in his kind, and therefore not only to content themselves that there is sufficient, but to foresee how they shall be able to obtain the same. Otherwise, as he that walketh London streets, though he be in the midst of plenty, yet if he want means, is not the better, but hath rather his sorrow increased by the sight of that he wanteth, and cannot enjoy it, so also there, if thou want art and other necessaries thereunto belonging, thou mayest see that thou wantest and thy heart desireth, and yet be never the better for the same. Therefore, if thou see thine own insufficiency of thyself, then join to some others, where thou mayest in some measure enjoy the same; otherwise, assure thyself thou art better where thou art. Some there be that thinking altogether of their present wants they enjoy here, and not dreaming of any there, through indiscretion plunge themselves into a deeper sea of misery. As for example, it may be here, rent and firing are so chargeable, as without great difficulty a man cannot accomplish the same; never considering, that as he shall have no rent to pay, so he must build his house before he have it, and peradventure may with more ease pay for his fuel here, than cut and fetch it home, if he have not cattle to draw it there; though there is no scarcity, but rather too great plenty.

_____ I write not these things to dissuade any that shall seriously,
1623 upon due examination, set themselves to further the glory
        of God, and the honor of our country, in so worthy an
enterprise, but rather to discourage such as with too great lightness
undertake such courses; who peradventure strain themselves and
their friends for their passage thither, and are no sooner there, than
seeing their foolish imagination made void, are at their wits' end,
and would give ten times so much for their return, if they could procure it; and out of such discontented passions and humors, spare not
to lay that imputation upon the country, and others, which themselves deserve.

As, for example, I have heard some complain of others for their
large reports of New England, and yet because they must drink water
and want many delicates they here enjoyed, could presently return
with their mouths full of clamors. And can any be so simple as to
conceive that the fountains should stream forth wine or beer, or the
woods and rivers be like butchers' shops, or fishmongers' stalls,
where they might have things taken to their hands? If thou canst
not live without such things, and hast no means to procure the one,
and wilt not take pains for the other, nor hast ability to employ others for thee, rest where thou art; for as a proud heart, a dainty tooth,
a beggar's purse, and an idle hand, be here intolerable, so that person that hath these qualities there, is much more abominable. If
therefore God hath given thee a heart to undertake such courses,
upon such grounds as bear thee out in all difficulties, viz. his glory as
a principal, and all other outward good things but as accessaries,
which peradventure thou shalt enjoy, and it may be not, then thou
wilt with true comfort and thankfulness receive the least of his mercies; whereas on the contrary, men deprive themselves of much hap-
piness, being senseless of greater blessings, and through prejudice
smother up the love and bounty of God; whose name be ever glori-
fied in us, and by us, now and evermore. Amen.

A POSTSCRIPT.

I F any man desire a more ample relation of the state of this country, before such time as this present Relation taketh place, I refer
them to the two former printed books; the one published by the
President and Council for New England, and the other gathered by
the inhabitants of this present Plantation at Plymouth in New
England.[1]

NOTES

DEDICATION (pp. 3-5)

[1] The merchant adventurers.

[2] This sentiment shows how little obnoxious the first settlers of New England were to the charge of fanaticism, which has often been alleged against them by persons alike ignorant of their spirit and their history.

[3] EDWARD WINSLOW was, according to Hutchinson, "of a very reputable family and of a very active genius" – "a gentleman of the best family of any of the Plymouth planters, his father, Edward Winslow, Esq., being a person of some figure at Droitwich, in Worcestershire," a town seven miles from Worcester, celebrated for its salt springs. Edward was the eldest of eight children, and was born at Droitwich Oct. 19, 1595, as appears from the following extract from the records of St. Peter's church in that place: "1595, Oct. 20, baptized Edward, son of Edward Winslow, born the previous Friday," which was the 19th. His mother's name was Magdalen; her surname is unknown; she was married Nov. 3, 1594. He was not one of the original band of Pilgrims who escaped to Holland in 1608, but being on his travels, fell in with them at Leyden, in 1617, as we learn from his Brief Narration, where he speaks of "living three years under Mr. Robinson's ministry before we began the work of plantation in New England." His name stands the third among the signers of the Compact on board the Mayflower; and his family consisted at that time of his wife, Elizabeth, George Soule, and two oth-ers, perhaps his children, Edward and John, who died young. As has already been seen, and will hereafter appear, he was one of the most energetic and trusted men in the Colony. He went to England in 1623, 1624, 1635 and 1646, as agent of the Plymouth or Massachusetts colonies; and in 1633 he was chosen governor, to which office he was reëlected in 1636 and 1644. He did not return to New England after 1646. In 1655 he was sent by Cromwell as one of three commissioners to superintend the expedition against the Spanish possessions in the West Indies, and died at sea, near Hispaniola, on the 8th of May of that year, in his 60th year. An interesting letter, written by him at Barbadoes, March 16, and addressed to Secretary Thurloe, is preserved in Thurloe's State Papers, iii. 250. Three letters of his to Gov. Winthrop, one to the Commissioners of the United Colonies, and another to Thurloe from Barbadoes, March 30, are contained in Hutchinson's Collection of Papers, pp. 60, 110, 153, 228, 268.

In 1637 he obtained a grant of a valuable tract of land at Green's harbour, now Marshfield, to which he gave the name of Careswell. This estate continued in the family till a few years since, when it came into possession of Daniel Webster, the late Secretary of State.

Edward Winslow's son, (2) Josiah, born at Plymouth in 1628, was governor of the Colony, from 1673 to his death in 1680, and commanded the New-England forces in Philip's war. (3) Isaac, his only surviving son, sustained the chief civil and military offices in the county of Plymouth after its incorporation with Massachusetts, and was President of the Provincial Council. He died in 1738, aged 68. (4) John, his son, was a captain in the expedition against Cuba in 1740, a colonel at Louisburgh in 1744, and afterwards a major-general in the British service. He died in 1774, aged 71. His son, (5) Isaac, was a physician in Marshfield, and died in 1819, aged 80. His only son, (6) John, was an attorney, and died in 1822, aged 48. His only surviving son, (7) Isaac, and the last surviving male descendant of Gov. Edward, of the name of Winslow, born in 1813, resides in Boston, and possesses original portraits of these his illustrious ancestors. See Mass. Hist. Coll. xxvii. 286.

Edward Winslow had four brothers, all of whom came over to New England. Their names were, John, born in April, 1597; Kenelm, born, April 29, 1599; Gilbert, born in Oct. 1600; and Josiah, born in Feb. 1605. – John came in the Fortune in 1621, married Mary Chilton, who came in the Mayflower, and removed to Boston, in 1655, where he died in 1674, aged 77. He left a numerous posterity, one of whom is Isaac Winslow, Esq., of Roxbury, formerly a merchant in Boston. – Gilbert came in the Mayflower, and soon left the Colony, and it is thought went to Portsmouth, N. H. and died before 1660. – Kenelm and Josiah arrived at Plymouth before 1632, and both settled at Marshfield. The former died whilst on a visit at Salem in 1672, aged 73, and the latter in 1674, aged 69. – Edward Winslow's

sisters were Eleanor, born in April, 1598, Elizabeth, born in March, 1601, and Magdalen, born Dec. 26, 1604. Elizabeth died in Jan. 1604, and neither of the other two ever came to New England.

For the copy of the record of St. Peter's Church, Droitwich, containing the births and baptisms of Edward Winslow and his sisters and brothers, excepting Josiah, I am indebted to Isaac Winslow, Esq., of Roxbury, whose son, Isaac, of New York, visited that place for this purpose in Aug. 1839. I am also indebted to Mr. Isaac Winslow, of Boston, for the loan of the family bible of the Winslows, containing on one of its covers an ancient register, corresponding nearly with the Droitwich records, with the addition of the birth and baptism of Josiah, the youngest child. See Hutchinson's Mass. i. 187, ii. 457 – 460; Belknap's Am. Biog. ii. 281 – 309; Mitchell's Bridgewater, p. 387 – 390; Deane's Scituate, p. 388 – 390; Thatcher's Plymouth, p. 90 – 103; 139 – 144; Morton's Memorial, pp. 178, 235, 259 – 261, 382, 415; Hazard's Hist. Coll. i. 326.

To the Reader (p. 6)

[1]At Wessagusset, or Weymouth, of which an ample account will be found in the ensuing Narrative.

[2]Thomas Weston.

[3]Winslow returned in the ship Charity, in March, 1624. He had been absent six months, having sailed from Plymouth in the Anne, on the 10th of Sept. previous. See Bradford, in Prince, p. 221, 225.

⁴This serves to confirm the statement of numerous typographical errors in the previous Narrative.

Chapter 1 (p. 7)

¹West had a commission as admiral of New England, to restrain such ships as came to fish and trade without license from the New England Council; but finding the fishermen stubborn fellows, and too strong for him, he sails for Virginia; and their owners complaining to Parliament, procured an order that fishing should be free. Bradford, in Prince, p. 218, and in Morton, p. 97.

²The Damariscove islands, five or six in number, lying west by north from Monhegan, were early resorted to and occupied as fishing-stages. See Williamson's Maine, i. 56.

³On the 22d of March, 1622, at mid-day, the Indians, by a preconcerted plan, fell upon the English settlements in Virginia, and massacred 347 persons. A war of extermination immediately ensued. See Smith's Virginia, ii. 64 – 79, and Stith, p. 208 – 213.

⁴Opechancanough, as the name is commonly spelt.

Chapter 2 (pp. 8-18)

¹The Narragansetts were a numerous and powerful tribe that occupied nearly the whole of the present territory of the State of Rhode Island, including the islands in Narragansett Bay. They had escaped the pestilence which had depopulated other parts of New England, and their population at this time was estimated at thirty thousand, of whom five thousand were warriors. Roger Williams says they were so populous that a traveller would meet with a dozen Indian towns in twenty miles. They were a martial and formidable race, and were frequently at war with the Pokanokets on the east, the Pequots on the west, and the Massachusetts on the north. See Gookin in Mass. Hist. Coll. i. 147; Callender in R. I. Hist. Coll. iv. 123; Potter's Early History of Narragansett, ibid. iii. 1, and Hutchinson's Mass. i. 457.

²"Since the death of so many Indians, they thought to lord it over the rest, conceive we are a bar in their way, and see Massasoit already take shelter under our wings." Bradford's Hist. quoted by Prince, p. 200.

³Canonicus, the great sachem of the Narragansetts, though hostile to the Plymouth colonists, probably on account of their league with his enemy, Massasoit, showed himself friendly to the first settlers of Rhode Island, who planted themselves within his territory. Roger Williams says that "when the hearts of my countrymen and friends failed me, the Most High stirred up the barbarous heart of Connonicus to love me as his son to the last gasp. Were it not for the favor that God gave me with him, none of these parts, no, not Rhode Island had been purchased or obtained; for I never gat any thing of Connonicus but by gift." In 1636 the Massachusetts Colony sent to him "a solemn embassage, " who "observed in the sachem much state, great command over his men, and marvellous wisdom in his

answers." Edward Johnson, who probably accompanied the ambassadors, has given in his "Wonderworking Providence," b. ii. ch. vi. a very minute account of their reception and entertainment. He says that "Canonicus was very discreet in his answers." He died June 4th, 1647, according to Winthrop, "a very old man." See his Life in Thatcher's Indian Biography, i. 177 – 209, and in Drake's Book of the Indians, b. ii. 54 – 57.

⁴Probably Stephen Hopkins.

⁵Isaac Allerton.

⁶"There is a remarkable coincidence in the form of this challenge with that of the challenge given by the Scythian prince to Darius. Five arrows made a part of the present sent by his herald to the Persian king. The manner of declaring war by the Aracaunian Indians of South America, was by sending from town to town an arrow clenched in a dead man's hand." Holmes, Annals, i. 177. See Rollin, Anc. Hist. b. vi. s. 4; and Mass. Hist. Coll. xv. 69.

⁷Bradford adds, "Which are locked every night; a watch and ward kept in the day." Prince, p. 200.

⁸This was the first general muster in New England, and the embryo of our present militia system.

⁹This indicates that the writer himself, Winslow, was one of the party.

¹⁰So early was the name of Gurnet given to this remarkable feature of Plymouth harbour. It is a peninsula or promontory, connected with Marshfield by a beach about six miles long, called Salthouse beach. It contains about twenty-seven acres of excellent soil. On its southern extremity, or nose, are two light-houses. It probably received its name from some headland known to the Pilgrims in the mother country. The late Samuel Davis, of Plymouth, the accurate topographer, and faithful chronicler of the Old Colony, says, "Gurnet is the name of several places on the coast of England; in the Channel we believe there are at least two." Connected with the Gurnet by a narrow neck, and contiguous to Clark's island, is another headland, called Saquish, containing ten or fourteen acres. See note 2 on page 164, Mass. Hist. Coll. xiii. 182, 204, and Thacher's Plymouth, p. 330.

¹¹The sachem of the Wampanoags.

¹²The same as Coubatant or Corbitant.

¹³What is now called a *brave*.

¹⁴We should like to have known more about this second voyage to Boston harbour.

¹⁵On the part of.

¹⁶This headland is Hither Manomet Point, forming the southern boundary of Plymouth bay. Manomet is the most prominent landmark in Barnstable bay, being visible from all points of its circling shore, from Sandwich to Provincetown.

¹⁷Brabbles, clamors.

¹⁸The passengers in the Fortune.

¹⁹Winslow himself had sent home too flattering an account of their condition.

²⁰"She brings a letter to Mr. Carver from Mr. Weston, of Jan. 17. By his letter we find he has quite deserted us, and is going to settle a plantation of his own. The boat

brings us a kind letter from Mr. John Huddleston, a captain of a ship fishing at the eastward, whose name we never heard before, to inform us of a massacre of 400 English by the Indians in Virginia, whence he came. By this boat the Governor returns a grateful answer, and with them sends Mr. Winslow in a boat of ours to get provisions of the fishing ships; whom Captain Huddleston receives kindly, and not only spares what he can, but writes to others to do the like; by which means he gets as much bread as amounts to a quarter of a pound a person per day till harvest; the Governor causing their portion to be daily given them, or some had starved. And by this voyage we not only got a present supply, but also learn the way to those parts for our future benefit." Bradford, in Prince, p. 202. Huddleston's letter, (or Hudston's, as Morton calls him,) may be found in New England's Memorial, p. 80. See note [3] on page 7.

[21]See note [2] on page 7.

[22]The burying-hill. The intelligence of the massacre in Virginia reached Plymouth in May, and was the immediate incitement to the erection of this fort. See page 7.

"Some traces of the fort are still visible on the eminence called the burying-hill, directly above the meeting-house of the first church in Plymouth. After the fort was used as a place of worship, it is probable they began to bury their dead around it. Before that time the burial-place was on the bank, above the rock on which the landing was made." Judge Davis's note in Morton's Memorial, p. 82.

Chapter 3 (pp. 19–30)

[1]"By Mr. Weston's ship comes a letter from Mr. John Pierce, in whose name the Plymouth patent is taken, signifying that whom the governor admits into the association, he will approve." Bradford, in Prince, p. 204.

[2]They came upon no religious design, as did the planters of Plymouth; so they were far from being Puritans. Mr. Weston in a letter owns that many of them are rude and profane fellows. Mr. Cushman in another writes, "They are no men for us, and I fear they will hardly deal so well with the savages as they should. I pray you therefore signify to Squanto that they are a distinct body from us, and we have nothing to do with them, nor must be blamed for their faults, much less can warrant their fidelity." And Mr. John Pierce in another writes, "As for Mr. Weston's company they are too base in condition for the most part, as in all appearance not fit for an honest man's company. I wish they prove otherwise." Bradford, in Prince, p. 203.

[3]Boston harbour.

[4]Or Wessagusset, now called Weymouth.

[5]Dr. Fuller.

[6]That is, the same Indians.

[7]This is supposed to be the same Jones who was captain of the Mayflower.

[8]Prince says, p. 205, that "Mr. Winslow seems to mistake in thinking Captain Jones was now bound for Virginia;" and Bradford states that "she was on her way from Virginia homeward, being sent out by some merchants to discover the shoals about

Cape Cod, and harbours between this and Virginia."

[9]"Of her we buy knives and beads, which is now good trade, though at cent. per cent. or more, and yet pay away coat beaver at 3s. a pound, (which a few years after yields 20s); by which means we are fitted to trade both for corn and beaver." Bradford, in Prince, p. 205, and in Morton's Memorial, p. 83.

[10]Isaac Allerton.

[11]Chatham.

[12]His disorder was a fever, accompanied with "a bleeding at the nose, which the Indians reckon a fatal symptom." Before his death "he desired the Governor (Bradford) to pray that he might go to the Englishman's God in heaven, bequeathing divers of his things to sundry of his English friends, as remembrances of his love; of whom we had great loss." Bradford, in Prince, p. 206, and in Morton, p. 85. Judge Davis adds in his note, that "Governor Bradford's pen was worthily employed in the tender notice taken of the death of this child of nature. With some aberrations, his conduct was generally irreproachable, and his useful services to the infant settlement entitle him to grateful remembrance."

[13]Aspinet.

[14]The country between Barnstable and Yarmouth harbours.

[15]The distance from Eastham to Plymouth by land is about fifty miles.

[16]With galled feet.

[17]The Swan. See page 20.

[18]Nauset, or Eastham, abounds with creeks. See Mass. Hist. Coll. viii. 155, 188.

[19]In the original, *saluting*; probably a typographical error.

[20]The part of Sandwich, which lies on Manomet river.

[21]"It is almost incredible, says Roger Williams, "what burthens the poor women carry of corn, of fish, of beans, of mats, and a child besides." Gookin says, "In their removals from place to place, for their fishing and hunting, the women carry the greatest burthen." And Wood says, "In the summer they trudge home two or three miles with a hundred weight of lobsters at their backs; in winter they are their husbands' porters to lug home their venison." See Mass. Hist. Coll. i. 149, iii. 212, and Wood's New England's Prospect, part ii. ch. 20.

[22]This is called Manomet or Buzzard's bay, though Winslow seems to mistake it for Narragansett bay, which is near twenty leagues to the westward. Prince, p. 208.

[23]"This creek runs out easterly into Cape Cod bay at Scussett harbour; and this river runs out westerly into Manomet bay. The distance overland from bay to bay is but six miles. The creek and river nearly meet in a low ground; and this is the place, through which there has been a talk of making a canal, this forty years; which would be a vast advantage to all these countries, by saving the long and dangerous navigation round the Cape, and through the shoals adjoining." Prince, p. 208, (A.D. 1736.) Mass. Hist. Coll. viii. 122.

[24]Oysters are still found in great excellence and plenty in Sandwich, on the shores of Buzzard's bay. See Mass. Hist. Coll. viii. 122.

[25]The common clam, (*mya arenaria*,) or perhaps the quahaug, (*venus*

mercenaria). The English call the former the sand-gaper, the word *clam* not being in use among them, and not to be found in their dictionaries. And yet it is mentioned by Captain Smith, in his Description of New England, printed in 1616. Johnson, whose Wonderworking Providence was published in 1654, speaks of "*clambanks*, a fish as big as horse-muscles." Morton too, in his New English Canaan, (1637) mentions them, and Josselyn, (1672) in his Rarities, p. 96, speaks of "clam, or clamp, a kind of shell-fish, a white muscle." Wood says, ch. ix. "clams or clamps is a shellfish not much unlike a cockle; it lieth under the sand. These fishes be in great plenty. In some places of the country there be clams as big as a penny white-loaf." See Mass. Hist. Col. iii. 224, viii. 193, xiii. 125, xxvi. 121, and Dr. Gould's Report on the Mollusca of Mass. pp. 40–42, and 85, 86.

[26]The razor-shell, (*solen*,) which very much resembles a bean pod, or the haft of a razor, both in size and shape. See Mass. Hist. Coll. viii. 192. Josselyn calls them "*sheath fish*, which are very plentiful, a delicate fish, as good as a prawn, covered with a thin shell like the sheath of a knife, and of the color of a muscle." And Morton says, "*razor fishes* there are."

"The animal is cylindrical, and is often used as an article of food under the name of long-clam, razor-fish, knife-handle, &c." See Dr. Gould's Report on the Mollusca of Massachusetts, p. 29.

[27]In Manomet river, as well as in Buzzard's and Buttermilk bays, are found fish of various kinds, such as bass, sheep's head, tautaug, scuppaug, &c. See Mass. Hist. Coll. viii. 122.

[28]He was the same as Cawnacome.

[29]"In their gamings," says Roger Williams, "they will sometimes stake and lose their money, clothes, house, corn, and themselves, if single persons." Gookin says, "They are addicted to gaming, and will, in that vein, play away all they have." And Wood adds, "They are so bewitched with these two games, that they will lose sometimes all they have, beaver, moose skins, kettles, wampompeage, mowhackies, hatchets, knives, all is confiscate by these two games." See Mass. Hist. Coll. i. 153, iii. 234, and Wood's New England's Prospect, part ii. ch. 14.

[30] Powow, a priest and medicine man.

[31]It seems as if the Captain went into Scussett harbour, which goes up westward towards Manomet. Prince, p. 210.

[32]In the Indian dialects.

[33]Or Iyanough.

[34]See note [21] on page 78.

[35]Or Pamet, now called Truro.

Chapter 4 *(pp. 31–39)*

[1] "All their refreshing in their sickness is the visit of friends and neighbours, a poor empty visit and presence; and yet indeed this is very solemn, unless it be in infectious diseases, and then all forsake them and fly." Roger Williams, in Mass. Hist. Coll. iii. 236.

[2]It was conjectured by Belknap, Am. Biog. ii. 229, and has since been

repeatedly asserted as a fact by other writers, that this person was the celebrated English patriot of the same name. But this is highly improbable. Hampden, who was born in 1594, and married in 1619, was a member of the parliament which assembled in January, 1621, and was dissolved by James in 1622, under circumstances and in a juncture of affairs which rendered it certain that a new parliament must soon be called. It is not at all likely that a person in Hampden's circumstances, a man of family, wealth and consideration, would, merely for the sake of gratifying his curiosity, have left England at this critical period, on a long voyage to another hemisphere, and run the risk of not being at home at the issuing of the writs for a new parliament. For the passage to America was at that time precarious; the vessels were few, and the voyage a long one; so that a person who undertook it could not reasonably calculate upon getting back in much less than a year. Winslow's companion, whoever he was, must have come in the Charity, which brought Weston's colony, unless we adopt the improbable supposition that this "gentleman of London" embarked in one of the fishing vessels that visited the Grand Bank, and took his chance of getting to Plymouth as he could. Now the Charity left London the last of April, 1622, and arrived at Plymouth the last of June. The visit to Massasoit took place in March, 1623, and after this no vessel sailed for England till the Anne, September 10, in which Winslow went home. Of course this "gentleman of London," must have been absent at

least eighteen months, which it is altogether improbable that Hampden would have done, running the risk of not being at home to stand for the next parliament, to which he undoubtedly expected to be returned, as we know he actually was.

Besides, had this companion of Winslow been the great English patriot, the silence of the early Plymouth writers on the point is unaccountable. On publishing his "Good News from New England" immediately on his arrival in London, in 1624, one object of which was to recommend the new colony, how gladly would Winslow have appealed for the correctness of his statements to this member of parliament who had passed more than a year in their Plantation. How natural too would it have been for him to have mentioned the fact in his "Brief Narration," published in 1646, only three years after the death of the illustrious patriot. Bradford, also, whose sympathies were all with the popular party in England, in writing an elaborate history of the Colony, would not have failed to record the long residence among them of one who, at the time he wrote, had become so distinguished as the leader of that party in the House of Commons. That his lost history contained no such passage we may be certain; for had it been there, it must have been quoted either by Prince or Morton, who make so free use of it, both of whom too mention this visit to Massassoit, and who would not have omitted a circumstance so honorable to the Colony.

Again, Winslow's companion was "a gentleman of London." Now

although John Hampden happened to be born in London, when his father was in parliament in 1594, he was properly of Buckinghamshire. Winslow, who was himself of Worcestershire, if he knew who Hampden was, would not have called him "a gentleman of *London*;" and we cannot suppose that this English gentleman would have spent so many months in the Colony without making himself known to its two leading men, Winslow and Bradford.

Equally unfounded is the statement that has gained so wide a currency and become incorporated with the history of those times, and is repeated in Lord Nugent's Life of Hampden, that John Hampden, in company with Cromwell, Pym, and Hazelrig, had actually embarked for America on board a fleet in the Thames, in 1638, but were detained by an order from the Privy Council. Miss Aikin, in her Memoirs of Charles I., ch. xiii., was the first to detect and expose this error of the historians.— For some of the views in this note I am indebted to the MS. suggestions of the learned editor of Governor Winthrop's History of New England.

³Probably the same which is now called Slade's Ferry, in Swanzey. Belknap's Am. Biog. ii. 292.

⁴Conbatant or Corbitant, was the sachem of Pocasset, and was subject to Massasoit. See Baylies' Plymouth, ii. 232.

⁵A neck of land in the township of Swanzey, commonly pronounced Mattapoiset, now Gardner's neck, situated between the Shawomet and Toweset necks. See Belknap's Am.

Biog. ii. 292, and Baylies' Plymouth, ii. 232, 234.

⁶"*Sachimmaacommock*, a prince's house, which, according to their condition, is far different from the other house, both in capacity or receipt, and also the fineness and quality of their mats." Roger Williams's Key, ch. xxii.

⁷*Wetu*, or *wigwam*. See Gallatin's Indian Vocabularies, in Am. Antiq. Soc. Coll. ii. 322.

⁸"There are among them certain men and women, whom they call *powows*. These are partly wizards and witches, holding familiarity with Satan, that evil one; and partly are physicians, and make use, at least in show, of herbs and roots for curing the sick and diseased. These are sent for by the sick and wounded; and by their diabolical spells, mutterings, exorcisms, they seem to do wonders. They use extraordinary strange motions of their bodies, insomuch that they will sweat until they foam; and thus continue for some hours together, stroking and hovering over the sick." Gookin, in Mass. Hist. Coll. i. 154.

"*Powaws*, priests. These do begin and order their service and invocation of their gods, and all the people follow, and join interchangeably in a laborious bodily service, unto sweating, especially of the priest, who spends himself in strange antic gestures and actions, even unto fainting. In sickness the priest comes close to the sick person, and performs many strange actions about him, and threatens and conjures out the sickness. The poor people commonly die under their hands; for, alas, they administer nothing, but howl and roar and hollow over them, and begin the song to the rest of the people, who all join like a choir in prayer to their gods for them." Roger Williams, in Mass. Hist. Coll. iii. 227, 237.

"The manner of their action in their conjuration is thus. The parties that are sick are brought before them; the powow sitting down, the rest of the Indians give attentive audience to his imprecations and invocations, and after the violent expression of many a hideous bellowing and groaning, he makes a stop, and then all the auditors with one voice utter a short canto. Which done, the powow still proceeds in his invocations, sometimes roaring like a bear, other times groaning like a dying horse, foaming at the mouth like a chafed boar, smiting on his naked breast and thighs with such violence as if he were mad. Thus will he continue sometimes half a day." Wood's New England's Prospect, part ii. ch. 12. See also Hutchinson's Mass. i. 474.

[9]Wood says, ch. 18, "They pronounce *l* and *r* in our English tongue, with much difficulty, calling a lobster a nobstan." Yet Roger Williams states, that "although some pronounce not *l* or *r*, yet it is the most proper dialect of other places, contrary to many reports;" and Eliot, in his Indian Grammar, says, "These consonants, *l*, *n*, *r*, have such a natural coincidence, that it is an eminent variation of their dialects. We Massachusetts pronounce the *n*; the Nipmuk Indians pronounce *l*; and the Northern Indians pronounce *r*. As instance:

We say	Anum
Nipmuck,	Alum } A Dog."
Northern,	Arum

See Mass. Hist. Coll. iii. 223, xix. 248.

[10]"When they are sick, their misery appears, that they have not, but what sometimes they get from the English, a raisin or currant, or any physic, fruit, or spice, or any comfort more than their corn and water, &c. In which bleeding case, wanting all means of recovery or present refreshing, I have been constrained, to and beyond my power, to refresh them, and to save many of them from death, who I am confident perish many millions of them, in that mighty continent, for want of means." Roger Williams, in Mass. Hist. Coll. iii. 236.

[11]The same as *pinse*. See page 13.

[12]Sokones, or Succonusset, now called Falmouth.

[13]Or Agawam, part of Wareham.

[14]Martha's Vineyard.

[15]"*Maskit*, give me some physic." Roger Williams's Key, in R. I. Hist. Coll. i. 159.

[16]"*Ketan* is their good God, to whom they sacrifice after their garners be full with a good crop. Upon this God likewise they invocate for fair weather, for rain in time of drought, and for the recovery of their sick." Wood's New England's Prospect, part ii. ch. 12.

Chapter 5 (pp. 40-52)

[1]Morton says, in his New English Canaan, ch. vii. "There are great store of oysters in the entrance of all rivers. They are not round, as those of England, but excellent fat and all good. I have seen an oyster bank a mile in length. Muscles there are infinite store. I have often gone to Wessaguseus, where were excellent

muscles to eat, (for variety,) the fish is so fat and large."

²The word *inclined* or *disposed* seems to have been accidentally omitted.

³Morton says, "this man's name was Phinehas Prat, who has penned the particulars of his perilous journey, and some other things relating to this tragedy." Hubbard states that he was living in 1677, at the time he was writing his History of New England. In 1662 the General Court of Massachusetts, in answer to a petition of Phinehas Prat, then of Charlestown, which was accompanied "with a narrative of the straits and hardships that the first planters of this Colony underwent in their endeavours to plant themselves at Plymouth, and since, whereof he was one, the Court judgeth it meet to grant him 300 acres of land, where it is to be had, not hindering a plantation." At the Court held May 3, 1665, it was ordered that land be laid out for Prat, "in the wilderness on the east of the Merrimack river, near the upper end of Nacook [Pennacook?] brook, on the southeast of it." Prat married in 1630, at Plymouth, a daughter of Cuthbert Cuthbertson. His heirs had grants of land in Abington subsequent to 1672. Drake says that after long search he has not been able to discover Prat's narrative. It was probably never printed. See Morton's Memorial, p. 90; Drake's Book of the Indians, b. ii. 35; Mass. Hist. Coll. xv. 78, xvii. 122.

⁴The notorious Thomas Morton, of Merry Mount, in his New English Canaan, b. iii. ch. 4, which was published in 1637, is the first writer who mentions a ludicrous fable connected with this execution, which has been made the occasion of some reproach on the first planters of New England. After relating the settlement of Weston's colony at Weymouth, he mentions that one of them stole the corn of an Indian, and upon his complaint was brought before "a parliament of all the people" to consult what punishment should be inflicted on him. It was decided that this offence, which might have been settled by the gift of a knife or a string of beads, "was felony, and by the laws of England, punished with death; and this must be put in execution, for an example, and likewise to appease the salvage. When straightways one arose, moved as it were with some compassion, and said he could not well gainsay the former sentence, yet he had conceived within the compass of his brain an embryon, that was of special consequence to be delivered and cherished. He said that it would most aptly serve to pacify the salvage's complaint, and save the life of one that might, if need should be, stand them in good stead, being young and strong, fit for resistance against an enemy, which might come unexpected, for any thing they knew. The oration made was like of every one, and he entreated to proceed to show the means how this may be performed. Says he, 'You all agree that one must die; and one shall die. This young man's clothes we will take off, and put upon one that is old and impotent, a sickly person that cannot escape death; such is the disease on him confirmed, that die he must. Put

the young man's clothes on this man, and let the sick person be hanged in the other's stead.' 'Amen,' says one, and so say many more. And this had liked to have proved their final sentence; but that one, with a ravenous voice, begun to croak and bellow for revenge, and put by that conclusive motion, alleging such deceits might be a means hereafter to exasperate the minds of the complaining salvages, and that by his death the salvages should see their zeal to justice; and therefore he should die. This was concluded;" and they "hanged him up hard by."

This story of the unscrupulous Morton furnished Butler with the materials out of which he constructed the following fable in his Hudibras, part. ii. canto ii. line 409.

"Our brethren of New England use
Choice malefactors to excuse,
And hang the guiltless in their stead,
Of whom the churches have less need;
As lately happened. In a town,
There lived a cobbler and but one,
That out of doctrine could cut use,
And mend men's lives as well as shoes.
This precious brother having slain,
In times of peace, an Indian,
(Not out of malice, but mere zeal,
Because he was an infidel,)
The mighty Tottipotymoy
Sent to our elders an envoy,
Complaining sorely of the breach
Of league, held forth, by brother Patch,
Against the articles in force
Between both churches, his and ours;
For which he craved the saints to render
Into his hands, or hang the offender.
But they, maturely having weighed,

They had no more but him of the trade,
A man that served them in a double
Capacity, to teach and cobble,
Resolved to spare him; yet to do
The Indian Hoghgan Moghgan, too,
Impartial justice, in his stead did
Hang an old weaver, that was bed-rid."

It will be observed that Morton mentions this substitution merely as the suggestion of an individual, which was rejected by the company. Even had it been adopted by them, and carried into execution, it would not have implicated the Plymouth people at all, nor cast the least slur on their characters or principles. For Weston's colony was entirely distinct from theirs, and composed of a very different set of men. Their character, as portrayed by Weston himself, and by Cushman and Pierce, before they came over, may be seen in note [2] on page 77, to which the reader is particularly requested to refer. Morton himself calls "many of them lazy persons, that would use no endeavour to take the benefit of the country." As Belknap says, "they were a set of needy adventurers, intent only on gaining a subsistence." They did not come over from any religious scruples, or with any religious purpose. There is no evidence that they had any church at all; they certainly were not Puritans. Neal says, in his Hist. of New England, i. 102, that Weston obtained a patent under pretence of propagating the discipline of the Church of England in America.

Grahame, i. 198, falls into an error in attributing this execution to Gorges's colony, which settled at the same place in the autumn of the same year; and Drake, b. ii. 34, errs in saying that Morton was one of Weston's company. Morton did not come over till March, 1625, in company with Wollaston, and settled with him not at Weymouth, but in Quincy. See Prince, pp. 221, 231. The accurate Hutchinson, i. 6, should not have made a fact out of the careless Hubbard's supposition, which the latter mentions as barely "possible." See Mass. Hist. Coll. xv. 77.

[5]Hansel, to use for the first time.

[6]The same as *pinse*, on page 13.

[7]Standish is said to have been a man of short stature. See Mass. Hist. Coll. xv. 111, and xviii, 121.

[8]When the news of the first Indians being killed by Standish at Weymouth reached Mr. Robinson, their pastor, at Leyden, he wrote to the church at Plymouth, December 19, 1623, "to consider the disposition of their Captain, who was of a warm temper. He hoped the Lord had sent him among them for good, if they used him right; but he doubted where there was not wanting that tenderness of the life of man, made after God's image, which was meet;" and he concludes with saying, "O how happy a thing had it been that you had converted some before you killed any!" Prince adds, "It is to be hoped that Squanto was converted." It seems Standish was not of their church at first, and Hubbard says he had more of his education in the school of Mars than in the school of Christ. Judge Davis remarks, "These sentiments are honorable to Mr. Robinson; they indicate a generous philanthropy, which must always gain our affection, and should ever be cherished. Still the transactions of which the strictures relate, are defensible. As to Standish, Belknap places his defence on the rules of duty imposed by his character, as the military servant of the Colony. The government, it is presumed, will be considered as acting under severe necessity, and will require no apology if the reality of the conspiracy be admitted, of which there can be little doubt. It is certain that they were fully persuaded of its existence, and with the terrible example of the Virginia massacre in fresh remembrance, they had solemn duties to discharge. The existence of the whole settlement was at hazard." See Prince, p. 226; Hutchinson's Mass. ii. 461; Belknap's Am. Biog. ii. 330; Morton's Memorial, p. 91.

[9]His bow.

[10]To England.

[11]"Thus this plantation is broken up in a year; and this is the end of those who being all able men, had boasted of their strength and what they would bring to pass, in comparison of the people at Plymouth, who had many women, children, and weak ones with them; and said at their first arrival, when they saw the wants at Plymouth, that they would take another course, and not fall into such a condition as this simple people were come to." Bradford, in Prince, p. 214, and in Morton, p. 92.

"Shortly after Mr. Weston's people went to the eastward, he comes there himself with some of the fishermen, under another name and disguise of a blacksmith; where he hears the ruin of his plantation; and getting a shallop with a man or two comes on to see how things are; but in a storm is cast away in the bottom of the bay between Pascataquak and Merrimak river, and hardly escapes with his life. Afterwards he falls into the hands of the Indians, who pillage him of all he saved from the sea, and strip him of all his clothes to his shirt. At length he gets to Pascataquak, borrows a suit of clothes, finds means to come to Plymouth, and desires to borrow some beaver of us. Notwithstanding our straits, yet in consideration of his necessity, we let him have one hundred and seventy odd pounds of beaver, with which he goes to the eastward, stays his small ship and some of his men, buys provisions and fits himself, which is the foundation of his future courses; and yet never repaid us any thing save reproaches, and becomes our enemy on all occasions." Bradford, in Prince, p. 216.

[12]"This may excite in some minds an objection to the humanity of our forefathers. The reason assigned for it was that it might prove a terror to others. In matters of war and public justice, they observed the customs and laws of the English nation. As late as the year 1747, the heads of the lords who were concerned in the Scots rebellion were set up over Temple Bar, the most frequented passage between London and Westminster." Belknap's Am. Biog. ii. 326.

Chapter 6 (pp. 53–56)

[1]The word no appears to be an error of the press.

[2]This allotment was only for one year. In the spring of the next year, 1624, "the people requesting the Governor to have some land for continuance, and not by yearly lot, as before, he gives every person an acre of land." Bradford, in Prince, pp. 215 and 226. See this latter allotment in Hazard, i. 100, and in Morton, p. 376.

[3]"But by the time our corn is planted, our victuals are spent, not knowing at night where to have a bit in the morning, and have neither bread nor corn for three our four months together, yet bear our wants with cheerfulness and rest on Providence. Having but one boat left, we divide the men into several companies, six or seven in each; who take their turns to go out with a net and fish, and return not till they get some, though they be five or six days out; knowing there is nothing at home, and to return empty would be a great discouragement. When they stay long or get but little, the rest go a digging shellfish; and thus we live the summer; only sending one or two to range the woods for deer, they now and then get one, which we divide among the company; and in the winter are helped with fowl and ground-nuts." Bradford, in Prince, p. 216.

[4]"At length we receive letters from the adventurers in England of December 22 and April 9 last, wherein they say, 'It rejoiceth us much to hear those good reports that divers have brought home of you;' and give an account, that last fall, a ship, the Paragon, sailed from London with passengers, for New Plymouth; being fitted out by Mr. John Pierce, in whose name our first patent was taken, his name being only used in trust; but

when he saw we were here hopefully seated, and by the success God gave us, had obtained favor with the Council for New England, he gets another patent of a larger extent, meaning to keep it to himself, allow us only what he pleased, hold us as his tenants and sue to his courts as chief lord. But meeting with tempestuous storms in the Downs, the ship is so bruised and leaky that in fourteen days she returned to London, was forced to be put into the dock, £100 laid out to mend her, and lay six or seven weeks to December 22, before she sailed a second time; but being half way over, met with extreme tempestuous weather about the middle of February which held fourteen days, beat off the round house with all her upper works, obliged them to cut her mast and return to Portsmouth, having 109 souls aboard, with Mr. Pierce himself. Upon which great and repeated loss and disappointment, he is prevailed upon for £500 to resign his patent to the Company, which cost him but £50; and the goods with charge of passengers in this ship cost the Company £640, for which they were forced to hire another ship, namely, the Anne, of 140 tons, to transport them, namely 60 passengers with 60 tons of goods, hoping to sail by the end of April." Bradford, in Prince, pp. 217, 218.

⁵This is the last time that Hobbamock's name occurs in the history of the Colony. His services to the infant settlement had been very important, and in the allotment of the land in 1624, mention is made of "Hobbamock's ground." In New England's First Fruits, published in London in 1643, he is described as follows: "As he increased in knowledge, so in affection, and also in his practice, reforming and conforming himself accordingly; and though he was much tempted by enticements, scoffs, and scorns from the Indians, yet could he never be gotten from the English, nor from seeking after their God, but died amongst them, leaving some good hopes in their hearts that his soul went to rest."

⁶David Thomson was sent over by Gorges and Mason in the spring of 1623, and commenced a settlement at a place called Little Harbour, on the west side of Piscataqua river, near its mouth. Christopher Levett says he stayed a month at Thomson's plantation in 1623. Afterwards, in 1626, or later, out of dislike of the place or his employers, Thomson removed to Boston harbour, and took possession of "a fruitful island and very desirable neck of land," which were afterwards confirmed to him or his heirs by the government of Massachusetts. This neck of land was Squantum, in Quincy, and the island which is very near it, has ever since been called by his name. It is now the seat of the Farm School. Compare Savage's Winthrop, i. 44, with Hubbard, in Mass. Hist. Coll. xv. 105; and see Adams's Annals of Portsmouth, p. 10, and Levett's voyage into New-England, in Mass. Hist. Coll. xxviii. 164.

⁷So called after himself, by Captain John Smith, who discovered them in 1614. He thus describes them: "Smyth's Isles are a heap together, none near them, against Accominticus." They are eight in number, and

are now called the Isles of Shoals. See a description and historical account of them in Mass. Hist. Coll. vii. 242 – 262; xxvi. 120.

[8]"Governor Bradford gives no hint of this third repulse." Prince, p. 219.

[9]The following is an alphabetical list of those who came over in the Anne and Little James.

Anthony Annable,
Edward Bangs,
Robert Bartlett,
Fear Brewster,
Patience Brewster,
Mary Bucket,
Edward Burcher,
Thomas Clark,
Christopher Conant,
Cuthbert Cuthbertson,
Anthony Dix,
John Faunce,
Manasseh Faunce,
Goodwife Flavell,
Edmund Flood,
Bridget Fuller,
Timothy Hatherly,
William Heard,
Margaret Hickes, and her children,
William Hilton's wife and two
    children,
Edward Holman,
John Jenny,
Robert Long,
Experience Mitchell,
George Morton,
Thomas Morton, jr.
Ellen Newton,
John Oldham,
Frances Palmer,
Christian Penn,
Mr. Perce's two servants,
Joshua Pratt,
James Rand,
Robert Rattliffe,
Nicholas Snow,
Alice Southworth,
Francis Sprague,
Barbara Standish,
Thomas Tilden,
Stephen Tracy,
Ralph Wallen.

This list, as well as that of the passengers in the Fortune, is obtained from the record of the allotment of lands, in 1624, which may be found in Hazard's State Papers, i. 101 – 103, and in the Appendix to Morton's Memorial, pp. 377 – 380. In that list, however, Francis Cooke's and Richard Warren's names are repeated, although they came in the Mayflower; probably because their wives and children came in the Anne, and therefore an additional grant of land was made to them. Many others brought their families in this ship; and Bradford says that "some were the wives and children of such who came before."

Fear and Patience Brewster were daughters of Elder Brewster. John Faunce married Patience, daughter of George Morton, and was father of the venerable Elder Faunce. Thomas Clark's gravestone is one of the oldest on the Burial hill in Plymouth. Francis Cooke's wife, Hester, was a Walloon, and Cuthbert Cuthbertson was a Dutchman, as we learn from Winslow's Brief Narration. Anthony Dix is mentioned in Winthrop, i. 287. Goodwife Flavell was probably the wife of Thomas, who came in the Fortune, and Bridget Fuller was the wife of Samuel, the physician. Timothy Hatherly went to England the next winter, and did not return till 1632; he settled in Scituate. Margaret Hicks, was the wife of Robert, who came in the Fortune. William Hilton had sent for his wife and children. George Morton brought his son, Nathaniel, the secretary, and four other children. Thomas Morton, jr. was probably the son of Thomas, who came in the Fortune. John Oldham afterwards became notorious in the history of the Colony. Frances Palmer was the wife of William, who came in the Fortune. Phinehas Pratt had a lot of land assigned him among those who came in the Anne; but he was undoubtedly one of Weston's colony, as appears from page 44. Barbara Standish was the Captain's second wife, whom he married after the arrival of the Anne. Her maiden name is unknown.

Annable afterwards settled in Scituate, Mitchell in Duxbury and Bridgewater, Bangs and Snow in Eastham, and Sprague in Duxbury. John Jenny was a brewer, and in 1636 had "liberty to erect a mill for grinding and beating of corn upon the brook of Plymouth."

Those who came in the first three ships, the Mayflower, the Fortune, and the Anne, are distinctively called the *old comers*, or the *forefathers*. For further particulars concerning them, see Farmer's Genealogical Register, Mitchell's Bridgewater, and Deane's Scituate.

[10]"Of 140 tons, Mr. William Pierce, master." Bradford, in Prince, pp. 218 and 220.

[11]"Being laden with clapboards, and all the beaver and other furs we have; with whom we send Mr. Winslow, to inform how things are and procure what we want." Bradford, in Prince, p. 221.

[12]"A fine new vessel of 44 tons Mr. Bridges, master." Bradford, in Prince, p. 220.

[13]"They bring about 60 persons, some being very useful and become good members of the body; of whom the principal are Mr. Timothy Hatherly and Mr. George Morton, who came in the Anne, and Mr. John Jenny, who came in the James. Some were the wives and children of such who came before; and some others are so bad we are forced to be at the charge to send them home next year.

"By this ship R. C. [i. e. doubtless Mr. Cushman, their agent,] writes, Some few of your old friends are come; they come dropping to you, and by degrees I hope ere long you shall enjoy them all, &c.

"From the general, [that is, the joint concern, the company] subscribed by thirteen, we have also a letter wherein they say, 'Let it not be grievous to you, that you have been instruments to break the ice for others who come after with less difficulty; the honor shall be yours to the world's end. We bear you always in our breasts, and our hearty affection is towards you all, as are the hearts of hundreds more which never saw your faces, who doubtless pray your safety as their own.'

"When these passengers see our poor and low condition ashore, they are much dismayed and full of sadness;

only our old friends rejoice to see us, and that it is no worse, and now hope we shall enjoy better days together. The best dish we could present them with, is a lobster, or piece of fish, without bread, or any thing else but a cup of fair spring water; and the long continuance of this diet, with our labors abroad, has somewhat abated the freshness of our complexion; but God gives us health, &c.

"August 11. The fourth marriage is of Governor Bradford to Mrs. Alice Southworth, widow." Bradford, in Prince, pp. 220, 221. Her maiden name was Carpenter, as appears from the following entry in the records of the Plymouth Church: "1667. Mary Carpenter, (sister of Mrs. Alice Bradford, the wife of Governor Bradford,) a member of the church at Duxbury, died in Plymouth, March 19–20, being newly entered into the 91st year of her age. She was a godly old maid, never married."

Chapter 7 (pp. 57-66)

[1]The meaning of the word Kiehtan, I think, hath reference to antiquity; for Chise is an old man, and Kichchise a man that exceedeth in age. —Winslow's Note.

[2]"They relate how they have it from their fathers, that Kautantowwit made one man and woman of a stone, which disliking he broke them in pieces, and made another man and woman of a tree, which were the fountains of all mankind." Roger Williams's Key, ch. xxi.

[3]Kautantowwit, the great southwest God, to whose house all souls go, and from whom came their corn and beans, as they say. They believe that the souls of men and women go to the southwest; their great and good men and women to Kautantowwit's house, where they have hopes, as the Turks have, of carnal joys; murtherers, thieves and liars, their souls, say they, wander restless abroad." Williams's Key, ch. xxi.

[4]Wood, in his New England's Prospect, ch. xix. spells this word Abamacho.

[5]See page 33, note [8].

[6]See pages 13 and 37.

[7]Or centaury – probably the sabbatia chloroides, a plant conspicuous for its beauty, which is found in great abundance on the margin of the ponds in Plymouth. It belongs to the natural order of Gentians, one characteristic of which is an intense bitterness, residing both in the stems and roots. The gentiana crinita, or fringed gentian, also grows in this region. See Bigelow's Plants of Boston, pp. 79 and 111.

"The greater centaury is that famous herb wherewith Chiron the centaur (as the report goeth) was cured at what time as having entertained Hercules in his cabin, he would needs be handling and tampering with the weapons of his said guest so long until one of the arrows light upon his foot and wounded him dangerously." Holland's Pliny, b. xxv. ch. 6.

[8]"Their government is generally monarchical, their chief sagamore or sachem's will being their law; but yet the sachem hath some chief men that he consults with as his special counsellors. Among some of the Indians

their government is mixed, partly monarchical and partly aristocratical; their sagamore doing not any weighty matter without the consent of his great men or petty sagamores. Their sachems have not their men in such subjection but that very frequently their men will leave them upon distaste or harsh dealing, and go and live under other sachems that can protect them; so that their princes endeavour to carry it obligingly and lovingly unto their people, lest they should desert them, and thereby their strength, power and tribute would be diminished." Gookin in Mass. Hist. Coll. i. 154.

[9]See page 31.

[10]"Upon the death of the sick, the father, or husband, and all his neighbours wear black faces, and lay on soot very thick, which I have often seen clotted with their tears. This blacking and lamenting they observe in most doleful manner divers weeks and months, yea a year, if the person be great and public.—When they come to the grave, they lay the dead by the grave's mouth, and then all sit down, and lament, that I have seen tears run down the cheeks of stoutest captains in abundance; and after the dead is laid in the grave, they have then a second lamentation." Roger Williams's Key, ch. xxxii.

[11]See note [21] on page 25.

[12]See page 26.

[13]"The most usual custom amongst them in executing punishments, is for the sachim either to beat or whip or put to death with his own hand, to which the common sort most quietly submit; though sometimes the sachim sends a secret executioner, one of his chiefest warriors, to fetch off a head by some sudden, unexpected blow of a hatchet, when they have feared mutiny by public execution." Roger Williams's Key, ch. xxii. See also page 15 previous.

[14]"*Mosk* or *paukunawaw*, the Great Bear, or Charles's Wain; which words mosk or paukunawaw signifies a bear; which is so much the more observable, because in most languages that sign or constellation is called the Bear." Roger Williams's Key, ch. xii.

[15]"Their powows, by their exorcisms, and necromantic charms, bring to pass strange things, if we may believe the Indians; who report of one Passaconaway, a great sagamore upon Merrimack river, and the most celebrated powow in the country, that he can make the water burn, the rocks move, the trees dance, and metamorphize himself into a flaming man. In winter, when there are no green leaves to be got, he will burn an old one to ashes, and putting these into the water, produce a new green leaf, which you shall not only see, but substantially handle and carry away; and make a dead snake's skin a living snake, both to be seen, felt, and heard." Wood's New England's Prospect, part ii. ch. 12; Hutchinson's Mass. i. 474; Morton's New English Canaan, book i. ch. 9.

[16]"There is a mixture of this language north and south, from the place of my abode, about 600 miles; yet within the 200 miles aforementioned, their dialects do exceedingly differ; yet not so but, within that compass, a man may converse with thousands of

natives all over the country." Roger Williams's Key, Pref.

"The Indians of the parts of New England, especially upon the sea-coasts, use the same sort of speech and language, only with some difference in the expressions, as they differ in several counties in England, yet so as they can well understand one anoth-er." Gookin, in Mass. Hist. Coll. i. 149.

Chapter 8 (pp. 67–71)

[1]In September 1609, Hudson ascended the "great river of the mountains," now called by his name, in a small vessel called the Half-Moon, above the city of Hudson, and sent up a boat beyond Albany. Josselyn says, that Hudson "discov-ered Mohegan river, in New England." See Robert Juet's Journal of Hudson's third voyage, in Purchas, iii. 593, and in N. Y. Hist. Coll. i. 139, 140, and 2d series, i. 317–332; Moulton's Hist. of New York, 213, 244–249; Mass. Hist. Coll. xxiii. 372; Belknap's Am. Biog. i. 400.

Postscript (p. 72)

[1]The former of the works here referred to is reprinted in the Mass. Hist. Coll. xix. 1–25; the latter has been reprinted by Applewood Books as Mourt's Relation: A Journal of the Pilgrims at Plymouth.

LaVergne, TN USA
21 October 2009
161531LV00001B/20/A